MW00873396

THE ADVANCED SHADOW WORK METHOD©

The Advanced Shadow Work Method (ASWM)

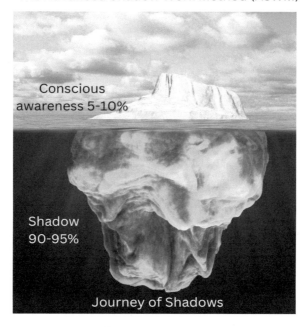

Conscious awareness 5-10%

Shadow 90-95%

Journey of Shadows

AUTHOR
COURTNEY KEISER

MA, Former Trauma-Informed Psychotherapist, Shadow Alchemist & Trauma Specialist, Reiki Master, & High Priestess

Copyright © 2024 Courtney Keiser

All rights reserved.

ISBN-13: 9798304379014

TABLE OF CONTENTS

Preface iii

Glossary of Terms ix

CHAPTER 1
THE CREATION OF A HOLISTIC APPROACH TO HEALING TRAUMA 1

Chapter 2
THE ADVANCED SHADOW WORK METHOD (ASWM) 27

CHAPTER 3
WHAT IS TRAUMA? 41

CHAPTER 4
BRIEF PSYCHOEDUCATION FOR GOOD MEASURE 57

Trauma and the Body 74

CHAPTER 5
INTENTION 81

CHAPTER 6
GROUNDING & COPING SKILLS 85

CHAPTER 7
THE POWER OF AWARENESS & SELF-TALK 103

CHAPTER 8
COMMUNICATION & BOUNDARIES 127

CHAPTER 9
THERE IS NO DESTINATION 141

Bibliography 149

Resources 151

About the Author 154

PREFACE

Despite a decade of studying, training, and utilizing a plethora of psychotherapeutic theories and techniques, I always felt limited by traditional therapeutic approaches. I kept noticing missing pieces in my clients' healing journey and experiences. It wasn't until I began to walk down my own path of shadow work that I discovered the healing magik[1] within the mystical path. The journey brought me further into enlightenment. It inspired me to create an approach that authentically supports clients in a holistic and well-rounded way—in mind, body, spirit, and energy.

I noticed certain clients in particular had difficulty feeling self-empathy, and had trouble speaking kind and loving statements to themselves. These were the missing pieces they needed to access in order to *actually* heal, but how? Clients weren't reaching long-lasting change or getting the answers they felt like they'd been trying to uncover for years in therapy. The clients who felt weren't in touch with their emotions, particularly

---

[1] When it comes to ancient words like "magik" I gravitate toward etymology and the origins, using the spellings that existed before the patriarchy and the Church fundamentally changed the English language. I see magik as a lifestyle and a state of being. It's a way of remembering that you inherently possess ancient wisdom and the power of creation. Magik is "consciously co-creating and choosing to live your life intentionally with awareness from a place of deep connection and service to yourself, the Divine, the collective, and Mother Earth for the highest good of yourself and the highest good of all."

their tears, couldn't forgive or love themselves. I knew there had to be another way to help them. I felt my clients and other seekers struggling to heal deserved more. I knew there was a comprehensive way to provide real, trauma-informed, holistic, healing and support. I also knew that I deserved more. I noticed I felt the same missing links. I decided to step out in courage and find a new way, just like you've bravely decided to walk down a new path by opening this book. You're a spiritual warrior yourself just for reading this far.

I've spent over a decade accruing the necessary wisdom to provide a comprehensive approach to healing using both scientific and mystical methodologies. That doesn't mean healing won't be hard work. I created this framework with a clear understanding of our innate, powerful nature to weave our own destiny. To become Wyrd, which means taking control of weaving one's own fate. Some of us may choose not to see a therapist for help, and that's a completely valid decision. If you're a self-healer and want to do this journey on your own, this book will help you succeed. However, at some point, you will likely need the help of professionals to point out your shadows, or what you can't see about yourself because it's blocked from your conscious awareness. You will understand this better later in the book.

Creating an approach that's tailored to self-healing might be putting myself out of a job, but I also believe that abundance flows through teaching that comes from the heart. I'll always have everything I need. Shadow work is complex, but it's worth it. **Embracing shadow work will transform your life if you want it to.** Let it. Surrender to it.

Although every individual's healing journey is going to look and feel different, **The Advanced Shadow Work Method**

(ASWM) honors your unique needs and experiences. I'll provide you with a plethora of grounding skills to choose from, with directives and steps that can be creatively attuned to you, because your framework is individualized. Through the one-of-a-kind guided meditation I created, we'll find the answers by speaking directly to your shadows. Speaking directly to shadow is a core part of my teaching, and it's a practice that I find mind-blowing, inspiring, enlightening, eye-opening, and shocking. It creates lots of feelings, especially the warm and fuzzy kind. This guided meditation separates my approach from other shadow or trauma healing frameworks, particularly combined with my unique perspective.

My hope is that by simplifying all of the wisdom, skills, and experiences I've had the honor of learning from incredibly talented and gifted healers, witches, therapists, mystics, and practitioners, that this method will give you everything you've been missing. I hope this book helps by giving you the answers you need to reach your goals and *finally* feel aligned to level up in your life.

Writing a book that involves sharing a holistic approach I've used over the last six years to heal my own trauma has been quite the quest. Initially, I didn't have any interest in the amount of work it takes to write a book, but Spirit had other plans. They told me I *must* write this book, relentlessly, and with a sense of urgency. I chose to listen to their guidance, leaning in, and here I am, a published author. Part of my journey while writing this book has been dealing with my own shadow response to the amount of work this process takes, and the emotional exhaustion of trips down memory lane to use examples from my own life. Writing this book also showed me where I still need healing.

My writing practice began with daily rage release full of wailing, sobbing, and guttural screaming. That would quickly transition to joyous gratitude and over-the-moon excitement. Overall, completing this book has been a wild ride of deep, transformative shape-shifting, raw, heavy, and messy inner work. I'm honored that I was guided down this path because it led me to the possibility of bringing clarity and profound healing to others through these words.

Spirit's desire was for me to arrive at this place within myself, accessing a wellspring of gratitude and unconditional love that I didn't know I existed. This year-long internal shedding and alchemizing of who I once was has pushed me to become a torchbearer of light for myself and others. It transformed me into who I am now: like Goddess Hekate, the torchbearer and guiding light in the darkness. I left behind a series of old beliefs: that I was evil, hated most people, that I'm a slut who can't be trusted, and that people needed to stay away from me. Now, I can see how beautiful and expansive my heart and soul are, and I no longer feel the need to hide them. I had to transform myself into the person I wanted to be, and someone I looked up to, so I could reflect the truth that others need to see within themselves.

In connection with the Age of Aquarius beginning on November 19, 2024, Pluto stations direct in Aquarius for the next 20 years. Completing this book is part of my mission and my purpose, and I know it's destined to be part of this revolutionary cosmic force of energy that's cascading into our lives. I feel very grateful, because I understand how important it is to be alive during this shift in the expansion of consciousness.

I'm honored to be a part of bringing awakening to the collective, and I'm sure many of you engaging with this text are part of that too. For all of you Indigenous peoples of all the lands, to the healers, mystics, light workers, heart expanders, witches, warlocks, visionaries, starseeds, empaths, ascended masters (like myself), conscious creators, awakened beings, environmentalists, sacred Earth guardians, animal and human rights activists and protectors, and the rest—I see you. Thank you for being here with me on this journey. I couldn't imagine doing this life without you all. I'm so deeply grateful for all of you.

If you don't know what the Age of Aquarius is, I will discuss it in more depth later. This book honors the energy and truth of the Age of Aquarius and the future we're moving towards. That future is one of love, higher consciousness, ascension to higher timelines, and experiencing life in new, unimagined ways.

To whoever is reading this, I hope you can finally feel truly seen. I hope you fall in love with yourself and all of your shadow parts. I hope you love all of your quirks and dark edges. I hope you know that you're so deserving of all the love and kindness in this world. All of that love and kindness already lives within you. I hope you can begin to see and feel the world as it truly is. I hope you feel full of wonder and magik, instead of trapped by the pain of your wounds. I hope you allow the world to teach you and surprise you as you grow and evolve with the changing seasons. I hope you feel empowered to go after what you want, to get what you want, to know that you deserve what you want—if it serves your highest good and the highest good of all. I hope you feel your fullest abundance and live out your wildest dreams.

Even though many of us have never met, I love you and I'm so proud of you for caring about yourself. For wanting more for yourself. For wanting to live in a brighter world. Thank you for your desire to wake the fuck up and learn how to weave your own destiny!

Each person that reads this book will create a ripple effect that emanates into every other life. Imagine the possibilities! I hope this book helps you heal and leave your trauma in the past, removing it from your DNA and genetic line. That may be triggering to hear now, but it will make more sense later. You're stepping into your freedom and ascension into higher consciousness and reality. Welcome! You can't unsee what you're about to see, so let's take off those rose-colored glasses now. You won't need them where we're going. The first step in this journey begins with honoring your physical body, and understanding that your beautiful temple actually tells you how to honor it daily.

GLOSSARY OF TERMS

Abilities: Several times in this book I refer to gaining greater abilities once stepping fully into my magikal life. I'm referring to Clair Abilities. This definition is not related to typical abilities like what most humans are capable of.

The Age of Aquarius: Refers to the astrological period when the sun is in front of Aquarius in the vernal equinox—which only happens roughly every 2,150 years—as well as Pluto stationing direct in Aquarius for the next 20 years. This is thought to be a time of increased spirituality, harmony, and a shift in consciousness from "I" to "all," bringing ideas and inspiration so people can live together in peace and equality.

ASWM (The Advanced Shadow Work Method): A methodology created by Courtney Keiser. ASWM classifies shadow as anything not in your conscious mind, which is 90-95% of your waking mind at all times. Within the shadow realm reside your shadow selves—or parts of you frozen in trauma, because they're unhealed—that become activated when you're triggered. Shadow selves project the past felt trauma onto the current, unrelated experience, but the individual is often unaware of the origin and assumes these deep, painful emotions are caused by and related to the current issue. Shadows can shape and color your emotions, actions, interactions, and behavior to drive you out of alignment with your truth. Emotions and reactions caused by shadow will feel extreme and out of control.

Shadow is made up of the subconscious and unconscious parts of your brain. Shadows also consist of shadow programming that extend to collective, generational, ancestral, and past life traumas transmitted as shadow beliefs or patterns that aren't derived from this life and aren't personal. Shadow affects you, your choices, how you show up in the world, how you relate to yourself and others, and your lived emotional experience. My approach looks at how each shadow affects the whole system and the areas it branches into, then, begins to program in new beliefs and behaviors as you heal from your wounds, releasing all that doesn't serve you and replacing it with what serves your highest good.

Akashic Records: The word *Akasha* is a Sanskrit word meaning "sky" or "ether," and its interpretation spans across many ancient cultures and religions. It exists in ether, or the non-physical plane of existence, the mental plane. Many experts, like master healer and teacher Linda Howe, consider Akashic Records to be an essential spiritual tool: "The Akashic Records offer empowerment and transformation by lending us exactly the wisdom, guidance, and energetic support that we need in this lifetime," (Howe, 2009).

Not just a tool, the "father of holistic medicine," Edward Cayce, considered the Akashic Record to be a warehouse of psychic information. "It can be equated to the Universe's super-computer system. The system acts as the central storehouse of all information for every individual who has ever lived on Earth. More than just a reservoir of events. It contains every deed, word, feeling, thought, and intent that has ever occurred at any time in the history of the world," (Cayce, 2020).

Ascended Masters & Teachers: Different from Akashic Masters. Ascended Masters and teachers are ones who have walked the Earth, but have ascended to a state of enlightenment. Beings that have chosen to take the task of helping us raise consciousness on a collective and individual level guiding us on our path.

Balanced Feminine Energy: This looks like being receptive, passive, contractive, intuitive, and inward energy (Note: Energies are genderless. Even though there are masculine or feminine expressions it doesn't correspond to gender—we all have both energies.)

Balanced Masculine Energy: This looks like being protective, active, giving, expansive, and outward energy (Note: Energies are genderless. Even though there are masculine or feminine expressions it doesn't correspond to gender—we all have both energies.)

Baseline: Refers to the "normal" resting state of brain activity. You are not triggered or in shadow. You are calm, grounded, safe.

Body Feeling Memory: These are held or unprocessed emotional and physical trauma physical sensations that remain in the body after a traumatic event.

Boundaries: Expectations of what you need from others in terms of space, communication, respect, time, actions, etc. Your boundaries determine how others can show up for you or support you in a way that honors what's in alignment with everyone's highest good. Boundaries help protect your sacred healing work by making sure you're meeting your own emotional and energetic needs with a supportive environment that's established through communication between the respective parties it affects.

Chakras: These are parts of the subtle body, made up of energy that include the mind and emotions, which can be affected by spiritual and psychic energy. Each chakra is an energy center in the body thought to be spinning wheels or disks that life energy flows through. There are seven main chakras running from the base of your spine to the crown of your head. These are thought to correspond to the bundles of nerves and major organs affecting our emotional and physical well-being. When chakras are out of alignment, or blocked, you have emotional and physical symptoms related to this. The seven chakras from the bottom up:

Root Chakra: pelvic floor—safety, stability, sexuality.

Sacral Chakra: stomach—emotions, intuition, pleasure.

Solar Plexus Chakra: above the navel—connection to divine, strength, power, your will.

Heart Chakra: heart space—acceptance, love, compassion, gratitude.

Throat Chakra: throat, mouth, ears—expression, voice, communication, creativity, inspiration.

Third Eye Chakra: between and above the brows—intuition, spiritual awareness, inner wisdom.

Crown Chakra: top of the head—spiritual connection, consciousness, and enlightenment.

Channeling: Someone who is serving as a conduit or channel for spirit to communicate through them in an altered state of consciousness.

Clair Abilities: *Clair* is French for clear. When you have a clear sense you can pick up more information. These are spiritual and psychic abilities that correspond with your senses. They provide the individual with abilities to communicate with spirit through one of these senses, creating meaning and understanding in the individual. Anyone connected to spirit will experience their connection and communication through one or many of these ways. Many healers have some of the following, I currently experience all eight with the most prominent being clairsentience and claircognizance:

Clairvoyance: clear seeing.

Clairaudience: clear hearing

Clairgustance: clear tasting

Clairsentience: clear feeling

Claircognizance: clear knowing

Clairscentence: clear smell

Clairempathy: clear feeling

Clairtangency: clear touching

The Collective: Refers to the population at large, as a whole.

Consciousness: Consciousness is related to the thinking, rational mind, critical thinking, problem-solving, and deductive reasoning. It can also span learning something new, focusing on a task you just learned, short-term memory, and capacity for alternative interpretations of complex or ambiguous data. Wishes, desires, and aspirations of our creative conscious minds only control cognitive behavior about five percent of the time.

Dysregulated Nervous System: This is when you're triggered or in shadow and are experiencing a state of imbalance in your nervous system. When your parasympathetic and sympathetic nervous systems aren't in balance. This happens from masking, unhealed trauma and shadow, suppressing your emotions to conform to expectations of society or not feeling your feelings and healing.

This can cause physical, psychological, and cognitive issues. Examples are: anxiety, depression, irritability, feeling depleted, trouble shifting out of negative emotions, pain, fatigue, seizures, bladder and stomach issues, changes in appetite, tense muscles or pain, inability to focus, memory problems, constant worry or fear, chronic stress, rapid heart rate, fainting, fluctuations in blood pressure, poor temperature regulation, tingling, numbness, excessive sweating, increased urination, migraines, and visual disturbances.

Eclectic Witch: This refers to a witch like myself who practices a variety of magikal and spiritual practices that personally feel good and natural to them at the moment. They're not tied down to any one practice or area. Many practitioners incorporate things like: Shamanism, Reiki, Eastern Philosophy, Yoga, Ceremonial and Ritual Magik, Divination, etc.

Flipping your lid: A term I was taught in grad school using the hand-brain model as a display to show what happens in your brain when you're triggered or you experience trauma, your conscious brain or your top lid (the neocortex which includes the hippocampus, amygdala, and prefrontal cortex) goes offline and your backup program or shadow brain (subconscious and unconscious mind) comes online, as these are the most ancient parts of the brain programmed to respond to danger.

The Four F's: When your nervous system is dysregulated or experiencing trauma and stress, one of the big four "F" responses kicks in as the previously conditioned and shadow programmed response to danger:

Fight: Taking action against a threat.

Flight: Running away from danger.

Freeze: Shutting down physically, mentally, and emotionally (also called dissociation).

Fawn: Coping with perceived danger by attempting to appease whoever is causing the danger to prevent them from causing harm. Also called "people-pleasing."

Guided Journey or Journey: This is a guided or led meditation to explore your inner world that allows enlightening information about you and your issues to be revealed. The concept stems from the Shamanic Journeying technique which take the individual into an altered state of consciousness through guided meditation and proceeds to traverse through Non-Ordinary Reality (also known as the Otherworlds) in search of spirit guides, lost soul parts, harmful entities, and symbolic insights in order to bring the troubled client back to homeostasis. This informed aspects of my shadow work guided meditation, but the process and goals are very different. I don't travel into the Otherworlds for my clients, rather I send them on a journey to uncover the truth.

High Priestess: As an initiated High Priestess of the Magdalena Rose Path it's important for me to share this definition because there's a lot of misinformation in the world. This is a role that *serves* as a sacred servant to the Earth, humanity and the divine. A High Priestess is a sacred keeper of ancient wisdom, rituals and ceremony, channeling the energy of the Goddess or divine feminine into practical experiences for her community. She raises the collective consciousness, becoming a frequency of divine love to help restore balance on the planet. She's accrued lived experience and deep wisdom in service, guiding ritual and ceremony, and has gained leadership skills and other exemplary qualities. She has studied and trained in magik. Her purpose is to gain experience as a spiritual leader, spreading the knowledge of the spiritual teaching she has learned and embodied. These guidelines help explain why writing this book is part of my mission and purpose.

Intention: A goal, purpose, or plan you intend to carry out and call into your life. It's about being mindful of your actions and understanding why you're behaving in certain ways.

Karma/Karmic Pattern: Karma is simply the opposite of what you're experiencing in a situation. It's the lesson, the balancing of the experience that will happen over and over again in the same life, or repeat in multiple lives, until the cycle is completed and the lessons are learned. It's not a negative situation that comes into your life as payback for misdeeds, as many assume. There's no such thing as retribution when it comes to spiritual truth.

Magik: I view magik (adjective) as a way of living and a state of being that's experienced when you begin to heal and love yourself, but I'm also referring to the experience you can have when ritual and a magikal lens are added into your life. The lens empowers you and it also inspires the desire to heal and become deeply connected with nature. Through this, you'll begin to remember more about who you really are. You are magik (noun), it's a miracle that you exist. Magik helps remind us that we possess ancient wisdom through the power of creation that is already within us. You create your reality.

Magik uses the spiritual wisdom you've accrued to create or manifest the reality you want.

I define magik (verb) as consciously co-creating and choosing to live your life intentionally with awareness from a place of deep connection and service to yourself, the Divine, the collective, and Mother Earth. Magik is the innate power and wisdom to intentionally work with Earthly elements of fire, air, water, earth, spirit, elementals, animal totems, and Gods and Goddesses to manifest and bring in their intention for your own highest good and the highest good of all. This is done through ritual, manifestation, actions, words, spiritual practices, ceremony, spells, meditation, intention, and connecting with nature.

Manifestation: In the context of magik refers to the act of bringing a desired outcome into reality through focused intention, positive thoughts, and actions using the power of your mind and making necessary physical changes in your reality to align with what you desire. The belief that your thoughts and energy can attract corresponding experiences into your life while also actively taking steps to align yourself with the energy of the thing you want through intentional actions, thoughts, and choices in energetic alignment with the thing you want.

Medium: Someone who communicates with spirit.

Natural Feminine Energy: This looks like unconditional love, understanding, nurturing, tenderness, kindness, emotional, allowing, creativity, feeling, stillness, flow, radiance, surrender, sensitivity, and ease. *(Note: Energies are genderless. Even though there are masculine or feminine expressions it doesn't correspond to gender—we all have both energies.)*

Natural Masculine Energy: This looks like confidence, inner strength, responsibility, focus, logic, support, stability, direction, protection, clarity, boundaries, courage, discipline, capable, assertive, and certain. *(Note: Energies are genderless. Even though there are masculine and feminine expressions it doesn't correspond to gender—we all have both energies.)*

Neuroplasticity: The ability of the brain to form and reorganize synaptic connections, especially in response to learning, experience, or following an injury. It's your brain's ability to adapt and evolve as you're rewiring and reprogramming it to do something that differs from how it previously functioned. We use this skill when we learn something new as an adult, like a new language, or how to play an instrument. It involves a lot of repetition, dedication, and patience.

Programming: This can be done through reading, writing, speaking, thinking, listening, and watching what caregivers, friends, and society models for us in behavior and beliefs. Through repetition, these cues become programs that create our beliefs, attitudes, feelings, actions, and ways of being that we subconsciously follow because it's conditioned into the shadow brain.

Regulated Nervous System: A nervous system that maintains balance between the body's fight-or-flight (sympathetic nervous system) response and its rest-and-digest functions (parasympathetic nervous system). Things that help regulate your nervous system include deep breathing, progressive muscle relaxation, mindfulness, meditation, spending time in nature, body movement, aromatherapy and restful sleep. If you practice coping and grounding skills, this state is within reach.

Reiki: An energy healing system used to bring an individual into harmony with the divine perfection of the self. This is done by connecting with the loving, balanced Source of life—whatever you believe that Source to be. Reiki works with our being at the quantum level of subatomic matter where our energy always seeks to express in balance and harmony. It can do no harm and it can vitalize all life forms. It's simply a balanced vibration from Source. It can speed healing and recovery and acts as a preventative tool for your health.

Reiki Master: Known as the Third Degree, this is the highest level of Reiki Master. The attunement opens the student to the full power of the Reiki energy. These energetic healers serve as a channel, or conduit, through which balanced energy frequencies flow from the Source of life to the person in need.

Ritual or Ceremony: In magik, this is a structured, symbolic set of actions designed to achieve a specific intention or outcome involving specific incantations and invocations, gestures, and sacred objects that are designed to channel energy and connect with spiritual forces to manifest desired results. It's a way to practice magik with purpose. Most people have heard about full moon circles or rituals.

Sacred Rage: Sacred rage release is done through screaming as loudly and intensely as possible while hitting either a pillow or your bed, or sticks on the ground outside. This rapidly moves emotion and shadow masks out of the way to reveal one's true feelings. It offers an opportunity to release these emotions in a healthy way without suppressing or shaming them. It releases the energetic emotion back into the Earth to be burned and transmuted into pure potential by the Earth's molten core.

Individual and collective oppression has always existed in societies affected by horrific, historical abuse and control. Through this process, we're giving the ghosts of the past, that are very alive within us, a voice to release what was never safe to release before. You're freeing everyone who has ever felt trapped or shut down. When you allow yourself, safely and consciously, to have an outlet for releasing your anger and expressing your truth without shame, it can ignite your courage to stand in your power. It will allow you to show up more authentically in your relationships.

Self-Talk: What you say to yourself. How you talk to yourself when you need encouragement, when you make mistakes, how you talk yourself up or down when stressed, anxious, or upset. How you narrate yourself in situations and relationships. How you feel emotionally and physically in your body as a direct result of what you say to yourself. 95% of self-talk happens outside of your conscious awareness.

Shadow: In the case of the ASWM, shadow is anything not in your conscious awareness and any thoughts, words, actions about self or others that aren't in your or their highest good and can even be seen as bad. This includes the wounded parts of yourself that experienced trauma creating false narratives and beliefs about you, others, and your experiences that color how you understand life. Your shadow also includes trauma from collective, generational, ancestral, and past life traumas. Shadows exist in your subconscious and unconscious parts of your brain, in your energetic body, and body feeling memory. Shadow creates emotional distress, nervous system dysregulation, physical illness and disease, phobias, and stagnation in areas of your life and relationships as a direct result of these hidden aspects of you, what was passed down, and your karma.

Shadow Program/Pattern: An umbrella term to identify a whole hidden belief system and program from your ancestors, the collective, or your past lives that doesn't just come from a shadow part of the self, because it doesn't seem to match up with your current life experiences. A shadow program is what the shadow part has programmed in through repetition of narratives, beliefs, actions, and emotions. The program becomes activated and turned on when that specific shadow gets triggered by a thought in your mind or an environmental trigger. Uncovering all the areas of hidden influence these shadow parts have on your behavior, thoughts, emotions, words, body language, energy, beliefs, actions, relationships, likes and dislikes is called shadow work.

Each shadow part creates a rooted network affecting various areas of your life that are seemingly unrelated, but are, in fact, shadow. All the areas affected would be influenced and chosen through the lens of that shadow without conscious awareness. We work to identify what those areas are and begin to reprogram what's actually in alignment with your truth in their place. Shadow patterns are created through generational, ancestral, collective, and past life trauma—anything that's been deeply ingrained over long extended periods.

Shadow Work: Doing the work to uncover what's hidden from your conscious view that's negatively impacting your life. This work will help you to better understand, love, and support yourself more fully. It involves excavating and unearthing the core of who you are, and releasing the old baggage that's been affecting your life that you no longer need. It means loving all the parts of you and understanding that the darkness contains the key to accessing your light and reaching full abundance. The work is learning how to honor all parts of your reality, feelings, emotions, and experience as valid and taking responsibility for releasing, learning, and healing without projecting it onto everyone and everything. This is a practice that empowers you and improves the overall conditions of your life.

Shaman: A trained and initiated person who has access to and influence in the spiritual realms. Their primary spiritual practices involve entering into a trance state during a ritual and divination for healing. Shamans are found in all cultures, but the most common Shamans in America are trained in Peru and South America.

Spirit: This word can take on many different meanings but for the purpose of this book I focus on any supernatural being or essence from another dimension. You may or may not know them.

Spirit Guides: Spiritual beings more evolved than humans taking on many different forms, including those you know as ancestors and deceased loved ones, or angels that offer guidance and support to a living person. They can help you navigate life's challenges and opportunities, and guide your thoughts and energy back to love. Everyone has them, but it depends on if the individual wants to believe in and engage with them, actively building a connection to obtain their guidance.

Subconscious: We are all utilizing about 50 to 60 percent of our subconscious mind at any waking moment. It remains largely unknown to our conscious awareness and influences our thoughts, emotions, and behaviors. The subconscious is the autopilot program that comes online where you don't have to think to do something, like breathing. Once we become conscious of it, we can change and control our breathing pattern. It holds all our backup programs regarding what was modeled for us in behavior, attachment, emotional regulation and coping mechanisms. Shadow and trauma live in the unconscious mind, and everything you've ever read, heard, felt, and experienced is housed here.

Toxic or Wounded Feminine Energy: Signs that you're stuck in wounded feminine energy or dealing with someone who is: victimization, powerless and weak behavior, patterns of manipulating others, withholding information, neediness, codependency, hypersensitive and overly emotional reactions. *(Note: Energies are genderless. Even though there are masculine or feminine expressions it doesn't correspond to gender—we all have both energies.)*

Toxic or Wounded Masculine Energy: Signs that you're stuck in wounded masculine energy or dealing with someone who is: abusing power, dominating, aggressive and controlling behavior, overly competitive, confrontational or defensive, criticising, avoidant, being unsupportive, and feeling unstable. *(Note: Energies are genderless. Even though there is masculine or feminine expression it doesn't correspond to gender—we all have both energies.)*

Trauma: Anything that happened to you that was upsetting, dysregulating, or experienced as danger and a threat to your safety, where you weren't protected from harm or taken care of. Trauma occurs when an individual isn't able to process or make meaning of what happened in a way that's helpful to move through the experience without blaming themselves. Unresolved trauma can be passed down through generations. Your ancestors, past lives, and the collective trauma influences our daily lives in seemingly hidden ways.

Triggered: When something in your environment, an event, situation, or person uncomfortably affects you into dysregulation. This looks like anxiety, stress, anger, frustration, irritation, sadness, loneliness or any intense emotions or feelings that aren't calm or at baseline.

Unconscious: Some studies have found that we're utilizing 30-40% of our unconscious mind at all times, but others postulate it's even more. Scientific estimates place 95% of brain activity as unconscious. This includes habits and patterns, automatic body functions, creativity, emotions, personality, beliefs, and values, cognitive biases, and long-term memory. In ASWM, I hypothesize that past life, generational, ancestral, and collective trauma are stored in the unconscious mind.

Window of Tolerance: This is your nervous system's ability to handle dysregulation without losing your cool, or being able to tolerate upsetting or triggering things. A large window means you have a "normally" regulated nervous system and have a regular coping and grounding skills practice that allows you more room before you feel triggered by upsetting things. It's why some people go straight to screaming (zero window of tolerance) and some can stay calm and talk through issues without wild swings of emotions (large window of tolerance).

Wyrd: An Old English concept that represents fate or personal destiny. This concept asserts that fate and destiny aren't an end-point, but an ever-evolving and changing path that you can bend and wield, taking destiny into your own hands based on the choices you make or actions you choose to take.

CHAPTER 1

THE CREATION OF
A HOLISTIC APPROACH
TO HEALING TRAUMA

I feel like there were hundreds of "aha" moments over the years, as pieces of the puzzle came together, addressing the missing links I kept observing in my work with therapy clients. I had a constant feeling of frustration with the limitations of traditional therapeutic approaches. I never really found a therapeutic approach that resonated with me fully. I'm an eclectic practitioner and an eclectic witch. I take valuable morsels that stand out to me from therapy, spirituality, alternative and metaphysical practices, and witchcraft, and put them together in my own way.

I feel a sense of awe and gratitude for the sheer scope of divine wisdom that exists, and a relief that our modern society is finally waking up to the value of it. I've done a lot of research to compile the beliefs and perspectives that function as the foundation of my work. My beliefs and perspectives are entirely my own, as in, they're separate from what was modeled, mutually shared, commonly known, or considered mainstream. I've created who I am (and remembered who I truly am) through the wisdom I actively pursued and remembered, along with what I downloaded from higher dimensions.

In my years of clinical experience, I noticed consistent themes popping up across all platforms, from private practice to psychiatric hospitals. Routinely, I was handicapped by systemic obstacles like paperwork, insurance companies, and general misinformation about trauma and how to navigate it. Regardless of whatever hurdles I encountered, it inevitably took longer to help clients make tangible progress in their healing journey. I was beyond frustrated by this.

Call me a perfectionist—or maybe I felt like there was more to the picture that others didn't or couldn't see. I noticed clients who had difficulty connecting to their emotions couldn't establish second-order change or long-lasting change. I discovered clients who couldn't access second-order change also had the inability to develop empathy for themselves. This was creating a psychological block that stopped them from utilizing loving self-talk that went deep enough to have an emotional impact. My mission became clear, I needed to create an approach that helped anyone achieve empathy for themselves that also helped them to understand the importance of self-talk. I felt it was my purpose to find a more accurate way to help clients access their shadows and trauma without getting stuck in them, or living under the lens of trauma for the rest of their lives. If we truly heal trauma that shouldn't be the case.

In short, it was my calling to discover a more effective way for people to heal and fully release trauma without packing that heavy emotional baggage around for no reason. Why the fuck are we carrying all of this baggage with us from life to life? I said, "No more, I'll make my own approach because the one I need doesn't exist. I may be the only one who sees the inherent need for this right now." So I signed myself up for the job. I'm trusting that I chose what was in my highest good even though it brought out all of my own shadows. I loved them, and raged out with them in frustration and anger, giving them a voice and an outlet. It's been cathartic, to say the least.

Another major "aha" moment was in my personal therapy with my previous therapist who also is a trained Shaman. (Of course, that's the type of therapist I would pick, since I walk with a foot in each realm.) As you can imagine, I'm not a great client because I try to therapize myself. She always knew when to reel me back in or invite me to see a whole perspective and angle that I'd missed. As soon as I saw it, tears would come. That's always how I know something is true at a soul level, it's an overwhelming sense of gratitude, validation, and love mixed with a deep ping of pain as I resonate with what I now understand. Part of it is seeing and acknowledging the shadow so it can be released. Discover what that ping of truth feels like for you. You will know it when you feel it.

Using Guided Meditation to Meet Your Shadow

While diving into my own shadow work, I tried using traditional approaches like Internal Family Systems (IFS), or parts work, along with the Jungian approach. I felt my trauma and shadow work through these methods remained too intellectual. I wasn't accessing my emotions because I was intellectualizing them. That's an easy trap—shadow can influence your perceptions when things stay too intellectual. I had trouble connecting to my shadow parts through the IFS lens in the way I wanted to.

My therapist suggested I ask my shadow a question, and then listen for a response. I think I squealed out loud when I heard a response back in my mind. I remember saying to my therapist, "Ummm, I didn't know we could actually speak to our shadow parts and they talked back! This changes everything!" A giant light bulb went off. I asked, "Can I borrow this idea and make it my own to work with shadow?" She said, "I would hope so, please do and please tell me how it goes!" That's when I knew I had to create a guided meditation to meet with the shadow parts, but I had no idea what that would look like.

I remember the first time I used this approach with a therapy client. To give full context, I had been working with this client for years leading up to this experimental exercise. I made sure to explain the whole situation and the risks. I checked for understanding and received consent. While this could be viewed as unethical to utilize a technique that's not board-approved, I was confident in my abilities, my role, and my skills. I had blind trust in the meditation working.

When I was using guided meditation with my client for the first time, I realized I could have a direct conversation with their shadow parts. That was a game changer. It allowed me to gather all kinds of information, and is what really sets this approach apart from other methods of working with shadow. My technique has already evolved quite a bit since I began using it six years ago, and as I become even more aware of its nuances, I continue to update and adjust the approach to reflect my understanding.

How Intentions Impact the Physical Body and Experience

Over 15 years ago, I read a groundbreaking book called "The Intention Experiment" by Lynn McTaggart. I was blown away that she was able to show scientific evidence of plants in various settings and scenarios responding directly to external stimuli, events, and most of all, intentions made to the plant. She connected her plants to lie detector sensors that measure water excretion in direct relation to intentions made, words spoken, and actions being done, proving there's undeniable evidence that plants have a direct reaction to human thoughts, actions, and their environment. Not only did it make me think about talking to my plants more, but if plants can respond this way, I began wondering how our body and nervous system are affected by the intentions we have and those around us as well? How do our thoughts and intentions change what happens within our bodies or in our environment?

While researching this, I came across Dr. Emoto's study of water[2]. His studies show that after intentions were thought or spoken to water, and it was frozen, the water molecules yielded various crystalline structures. One group of molecules was addressed with good intentions, love, and positivity, the other with bad intentions and evil or ugly thoughts, and the last group was ignored entirely. At the end of the testing period, when examined under a microscope, the group whose crystalline structures were the most irregular, chaotic, inorganically shaped and not aligned with sacred geometric patterns were the group he ignored. The group addressed with negative or evil intentions showed structures that looked like molecules of a deadly virus. Finally, the molecular group that was showered with positive intentions showed crystalline structures with beautiful sacred geometric patterns like snowflakes. Dr. Emoto discovered that water is programmable. It has direct reactions to its environment, intentions, thoughts, actions, level of attention, and words. Learning this led me to another "aha" moment. If we're made up of close to 70% water in our bodies, and we know that water reacts directly to intentions, thoughts, words, actions, then let's do some deep breathing and take an honest look at ourselves. Do you feel in your body the words that you speak and think about it? How much of what is happening in your body do you think you created and brought into reality through repetition? Or, do you think you noticed and named things you're self-conscious about and your body changed

---

[2] Additional information regarding his work is included in the Resources section.

form to reflect those very things? I was a full believer if I hadn't been one before.

I began to comprehend the incredible power and force that is our mind. I always felt that thoughts and intentions were reflected and held in the body. Yet another "aha" moment came along when I was at the witch school run by Intuitive Adviser Mia Banducci, aka Mia Magik, and learned beauty magik. We were programming the water in our body for self-care and self-love, beauty, and whatever else we desired. Mia's words about Dr. Emoto's study were astounding. I'd never had a teacher who talked about the same things I'd been passionate about for years. Sometimes, I felt like the only one who saw how profound these discoveries were, and how important they are as the science to back up what we intuitively know. It dawned on me that incorporating magik into activities that might otherwise be averted by most people could actually give self-love and body-positivity practices a chance to work. It sounds fun! And who doesn't want to see if they can speak their incredible future body into existence? I believe this practice can work, and the intentions I used to transform my own body are evidence of this.

Now that I was able to understand some of the ways in which our body, water, and mind are programmed by our thoughts, intentions, and environment—and how it directly impacts many people's self-talk, narratives, beliefs, how they feel in their body, and how their body reflects that—it all became very *real*.

Being able to approach clients working through shadows of low self-worth and body issues in a modern way that's fun, surprising, challenging, inspiring, and empowering felt incredibly powerful. It directly connects a client to their divine magik and power as a result. Witnessing how my body has transformed through self-talk and daily beauty magik has been a fascinating test run. Practicing these routines has, at least in my own eyes, made me appear more beautiful, healthy, and fit. It taught me to love my body anyway. It didn't matter what it looked like. It is whatever I made it. The more I valued and loved my body and myself, the more I wanted to take better care of my health and body. It's a great way to start building a client's awareness around self-talk that supports a path to self-love and body positivity.

As the water journey continued, I learned more about various studies being done on water that showed even more evidence that it can be programmed. German scientists discovered water holds memories of places it has traveled through. It can even connect people with sources of information when drinking this water. Also, tears hold unique memories of an individual as they've emerged from the body's storehouse of water; tears host a complete catalog of information linked to individual experience. Spiritual science is emerging at a rapid rate to factually back up what people connected to higher spiritual realms of information believe.

I realized that not only is our body programmable, but that we could heal it, and program it to reflect what we want it to feel, see, or experience—up to a point, within obvious limitations like the third dimension. This means you can't grow a third arm, but you could make your arms look more toned.

The power of spoken word and intention became ever more clear to me. It was the defining factor blocking many of my clients from fully tapping into their abundance. It made me realize there's a correct equation for grounding, self-talk, and loving, helpful thoughts that are supportive. Intentional thoughts and the spoken words you and your shadow need to hear are additional important elements.

This "aha" moment about water and intentions dovetailed with the knowledge I'd gained from my Reiki Master Teachings about how energy flows or becomes blocked. When trauma is stored it affects the body's ability to function and heal. The truth is, whatever you think and do is what manifests. Emotions are meant to be felt and then released out of the body into the Earth to be transmuted. But we were taught to repress our emotions, which means we store them in the body rather than move through them. Most—if not all—of our ancestors over roughly the past thousand years also did this. They unknowingly passed down whatever trauma they'd repressed into the next generation. When you don't feel your emotions, they manifest as physical illness, because your energetic system is clogged or in disharmony.

Most people know they want a loving and abundant life but are still thinking and telling themselves just the opposite. I've done this too, and one of the most frustrating and difficult parts is surrendering to loving yourself by being kind. I fought like hell to hate myself longer and stay angry. I was annoyed that I had to love myself to heal.

I now had reinforcement from Reiki teachings for the theories I'd hypothesized earlier—that generational, ancestral, past life, and collective trauma did, in fact, manifest over time in the form of hereditary chronic physical and mental ailments. I believe this is a result of stored trauma that's connected to where that emotion or belief lives in the body, particularly areas that tend to store that specific type of emotion based on their respective chakras and organs. Later, I'll discuss how Dr. Lipton's findings show that genetics can be changed and altered immediately by changing one's perception and environment. You can literally erase the trauma from your DNA.

For example, say your ancestor was a snitch, lived a life devoid of integrity, and his throat was slit in a past life as a consequence. The throat chakra will be affected in all future generations until someone breaks the cycle and heals it. Following generations had trouble with achieving abundance, speaking up, or stepping into their power and purpose. Genetically, the family has long dealt with throat issues like laryngitis, strep throat, asthma, overeating, smoking, COPD, and lung issues. Some members of the family openly express feelings of low self-worth, emotional disempowerment, lack of confidence, trouble speaking up, trouble living with integrity, and involvement in cyclical toxic relationships. Below, I have included Instagram posts I created to illustrate how energy is channeled or blocked in the body due to trauma, and what those blockages do over time. Imagine the impact these cycles have over generations.

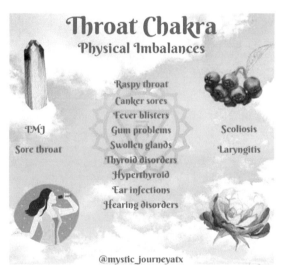

Fig. 10. & Fig. 11. Images on Instagram created by @journeyofshadows (formerly @mystic_journeyatx)

These imbalances are so hidden in the background that you wouldn't become aware of them on your own. They're buried so deeply, because they've been repeatedly programmed over many generations. Now, a hidden thought is being expressed as physical illness, a physical representation of the original trauma that happened to your ancestor that they repressed. This is why we need to do some of this work with professionals, who can help us access what we don't have conscious access to. I'm not a doctor and this is not medical advice. I'm providing you with evidence and theories that have resonated with me—use your own discernment to parse them.

Collective healing happens as a byproduct of our own personal healing. I believe that when we heal ourselves, we heal our deceased, living, and future relatives as well. When we heal, our unique energetic signature begins to vibrationally attune to higher frequencies. As we heal, each shedding and rebirth allows us to level up. Your conscious vibrational frequency is always rippling out into the collective and the universe.

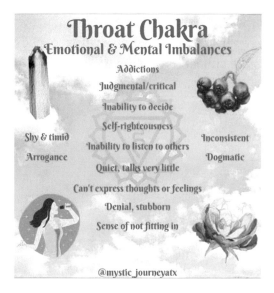

Fig. 12 & Fig. 13. Images on Instagram created by @journeyofshadows (formerly @mystic_journeyatx)

When we begin healing ourselves, that energy is felt by those close to us and it unconsciously affects the vibration of the collective experience. Maybe you look happier and healthier, and that's what initially intrigues others. You seem calm and things are going well. You're becoming more emotionally mature and intelligent. People are going to start asking questions about what you did. They will feel it, see it, and want it for themselves, too. Because not only does it keep rippling out into the human social circles you're connected to, but it ripples out into the collective consciousness, and is unconsciously healing on that level as well

Here's the real kicker, your own healing also heals and breaks the chains for your deceased relatives and future generations. That's right, your lineage will no longer be born with this baggage you and your family have been lugging around for decades or even centuries. That's a huge responsibility that I wish everyone gladly took on. Back to my point, it only has to start with you. You doing the work is all you need. The rest will follow.

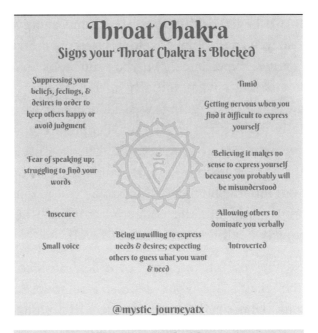

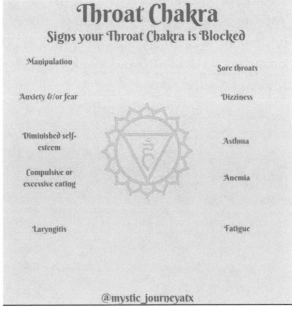

Fig. 14. & Fig. 15. Images on Instagram created by @journeyofshadows (formerly @mystic_journeyatx)

How Magik Transformed My Life and How I Help Others

After years of dedicated learning and prioritizing my education, I finally had all the tools I needed. Once I completed my year-long Priestess school training to become an initiated High Priestess of The Magdalena Rose Path, I retired my therapy license to work as a spiritual life coach instead. I had an "aha" moment when I realized: I'd fully trusted the process and leaned into what my intuition and spirit were guiding me to do. I studied the topics I'd wanted to know more about for years, and learned these skills so I could provide further teaching on them as a service to others. In my mind, my continuing education allowed me to create the most mystical, healing, rewarding, and fun job in the world.

In this year-long priestess school we were trained extensively in guided meditations, journeys, forms of ceremony, ritual, magikal ancient wisdom and teachings, and working with Gods and Goddesses in healing and craft. I was also diving deep into alternative practices for healing and connecting to divine feminine energy, power, and magik. I learned to release blocks and energetic holds from past lives. I was trained to lead sacred ceremonies as a mystic guide and healer.

These practices deepened my knowledge of meditation and took my studies further, weaving this sacred wisdom into the guided meditation I use as a framework today to help clients heal. These deep meditation practices help transport clients to another world. Even if they have trouble visualizing or meditating, they will see their shadow and have an experience. This is where my magik lives and shines bright. They will see their shadow vividly and hear it speaking to them. I know it to be true, and so it is. And that's exactly what happens. Through the power of my mind and voice, so may it be, as it is for your highest good and the highest good of all.

As I began working with clients under my new coaching business, I suddenly realized I had created something unique. Something that felt super special and different from other approaches. At first, I didn't fully realize all the ways my skills and wisdom would apply to my approach working with clients. Fast-forward to the present moment, where it all comes together to form **The Advanced Shadow Work Method, a holistic, full-scope coaching, mentoring, and counseling practice that derives from multiple schools of thought, perspectives, and techniques**. We address an issue's root cause, which will activate the client's key—or their innate ability to heal themselves—and initiate a process of alchemizing that transforms their entire mind, body, and spirit system. I don't do bandaids like your doctor gives you. Clients come to me to get real when they realize there's so much more to life than what's on the surface.

I've been on my healing journey for over 15 years. I've worked with therapists trained in: CBT (Cognitive Behavioral Therapy), Group Therapy, Trauma-Informed, Mindfulness Behavioral Cognitive Therapy, Transpersonal, IFS (Internal Family Systems), and spiritual therapy to name just a few. Never would I have imagined that my deepest, most powerful, profound, transformational, and truly alchemical healing experiences would be led by witches, healers, mystics, and priestesses in magikal ritual settings, not in traditional credentialed therapy sessions with trauma-informed mental health professionals. The contrast made me question all of my choices. I was a little bit bitter, but also no longer felt the need to conform to my previous career's limitations. I felt freedom in self-exploration, to find the tools and practices that would truly help others discover the key to their healing. These powerful, Wyrd women were the ones to hand me the keys. I'm so beyond grateful to all of you. I feel honored to pass this wisdom on. I love you. You know who you are.

The universe was having a grand time challenging my shadow of ego when I was attending all of these various witch schools, groups, rituals, and workshops to heal, expand, and grow spiritually and magikally. While I was working to step into more of a healer and mystic role, the actual challenge was to be open-minded, receptive, non-judgmental, and trusting. This was difficult because I'd worked for my entire therapeutic professional career in trauma. I had painstakingly completed graduate school coursework and over 3,000 internship hours; I'd spent thousands of dollars to acquire a professional license that said I was qualified and certified to work in trauma. Yet, these impressive powerful Queens, Witches, and Divine Goddesses who were *not* trauma certified made me forget I was pissed off and dwelling in my wounded shadowed ego about it. I was bitter. I thought: W*hy did I go to school if anyone could do this work and make a bigger difference than all the therapists I know?*

When I surrendered, and allowed others to heal me—whether they had a trauma-informed degree and student loan debt or not—I was able to alchemize my bitterness in an illuminating way. My whole black-and-white world cracked wide open into technicolor. I remembered that old adage that everything happens for a reason. My path was sacred, providing me with valuable skills and knowledge of the mind, body, and spirit that I needed in my tool belt to be the best healer I could be. I began leaning into gratitude and appreciation instead of anger, bitterness, and jealousy. That was transformative in itself. Every step of my journey was important.

These women provided me with such life-altering, profound healing that it leveled me up spiritually in my abilities, career, and life transitions. It was incredible. The tools that shape-shifted my reality were the guided meditation journeys in ritual space, magikal exploration, and shadowed discoveries of my past lives. I was able to come back into my body through somatic practices like sacred rage release, shaking, and dancing.

For the first time in my life, at age 30 (I'm now 36), I felt like I finally learned how to ground myself and move through anger. I could cry easily, but not about my stuff unless I was having a pity party. I could speak about anything without crying, not showing any emotion whatsoever. Sacred rage release has been the guiding light in my life ever since I started utilizing it to strip the shadow mask away to reveal the truth underneath.

Now, I can't imagine not using it. I get so excited to introduce people to sacred rage. To help women tap into their deep, dark feminine energy to embrace the powerful fire of release and break free is unlike anything else. When I began helping clients who couldn't feel empathy for themselves, I was able to help them access it through guided meditation. If that was not achieved or the desired goal was not met, we would do a sacred rage release exercise. In any form, rage release can help clients tap into blocked emotions and the truth.

"Xena: Warrior Princess" and my Shamanic Healing

Recently, I had another "aha" moment about my favorite TV show growing up, "Xena: Warrior Princess." Once I saw it, I couldn't believe I hadn't noticed before. When other girls my age were playing with dolls and watching cartoons, I was watching Xena and feeling deeply connected to the storyline of ancient times where Gods, Goddesses, and mythical beings roamed the Earth. I lived and breathed this show.

I was unconsciously programmed to see shadow because of this show. I learned incredible wisdom and spiritual teachings far beyond what a third-grader typically understands. The entire premise of the show is based on Xena's past traumas coming back to haunt her[3]. They provide her with an opportunity to choose her shadowed past, or choose her light and walk down a bright new path in every episode. It showcased an empowered, strong, dominant, badass, independent, warrior, and heroine who bravely chose to walk in her light through every test of the soul. I witnessed the incredible ability to alchemize and transform ourselves through radical self-acceptance and love. By loving and accepting her darkness, Xena was reborn.

During my last shamanic healing session, we retrieved a part of my soul from the Underworld. It had been killed during a war in a different universe. I was an immortal ascended master, a Goddess, and I had been fighting a monster that ripped my whole throat out (literally, we asked for clarification). It killed me, which wasn't supposed to be possible. I fought this thing for centuries until I gave up, creating a soul contract with it. My ascended masters who were there confirmed. My throat was ripped out, taking my light with it.

The retrieved part of my soul looked ethereal (I could see her in my mind's eye as the Shaman described her), glowing

---

[3] In the show, Xena murdered thousands of people. She does atrocious things and works every day to love and accept herself anyway. That's the Goddess Kali Ma's strength, will, and power. She is the ferocious loving mother. Her face is tattooed on my stomach as a reminder of my power. She's an iconic teacher and has saved my life many times. Look her up.

blindingly white. She was more radiant and beautiful than a human, like a Goddess version of me. She gave me my light back on a pendant necklace that was brighter than the whitest white light you've ever seen. Tears began streaming down my face. I knew what this was. It was Source light. It was the light of God. Universal consciousness light, or whatever you want to call it, was now within me.

I'd felt so far away from this before. I realized that I'd always secretly believed I was evil. I enjoyed the darkness of my soul, and enjoyed saying I hated people, even though my job was to help people. I thought I would hurt people and that they needed to stay away from me. I never thought I would ever love myself or feel unconditional love for anyone else. For the first time in what truly felt like eons, I could feel the warmth of this light radiating within me. It was a lot to take in. It was uncomfortable, and my resistance and immediate shadow program to reject it was painful.

In retrieving this part of my soul, we ended the past soul contract by writing it down and burning it. Then, I wrote a new soul contract that honors the abundant, powerful light and love that I possess. I now had the hard job of working to become aware of my shadow programs—the thoughts, beliefs, emotions, and perceptions that were previously hidden from view. I began to reprogram my mind to resonate with my light, love, and gratitude so that I could finally receive the abundance that I had deserved for so many *eons*.

This past life had blocked me spiritually, emotionally, and physically when it came to the empowered characteristics of the throat chakra—my self-expression, being heard, seen, confident, empowered, sharing my voice with the world, speaking my wisdom, being in my magik, stepping into healing others, being in my mission, fully stepping into love, and living my purpose. I felt how blocked I was while writing this book, and that's why I scheduled the Shamanic healing in the first place. This was a form of self-expression that I'd been energetically blocked from until now. Sometimes I still feel blocked in these areas, but that's only because of the mind prison I'd created up to this point. As time passes, it all becomes easier. Especially as the abundance has begun to roll in just as my ascended masters and teachers told me it would. I feel extremely grateful to have received this wisdom and healing.

To put it into perspective, that final healing was four months after I began writing this book. It took five more months to complete it. As I finished the book my abundance and love began to roll in, in *big* ways! It's hard to describe the joy I felt and am still feeling. If that doesn't reveal something about how deep this could go for you and your shadows, I'm not sure what else can. I'm sharing my wisdom and experiences because I want anyone reading this to know that if you're blocked, and you think you've tried everything—you haven't. There's so much more going on with you than what our current life's conscious awareness and society at large are going to reveal to you. So please, look into Shamanic healing or past life, ancestral, and generational healing because you deserve to be free in this life and to experience living with a clean slate. Then, do shadow work to reprogram any old hidden stories that are keeping you stuck in the same place, energy, and vibration.

After connecting my Shamanic healing experiences with Xena as a lens, I can understand why I resonated so much with a timeline where monsters and Gods and Goddesses existed, because it felt like home. I'm technically a human in this life, but I've never been human and I don't come from Earth. The validation and peace I felt from learning that truth increased my capacity for acceptance in my experiences and feelings.

Growing up, I felt like an alien walking around in a joke of a reality because of how asleep and programmed people are. So many people operate like robots without their own thoughts, listening to and believing in whatever outlandish, nonsensical lies the government, media, and pop culture tells them. People care about filling their brains with everything that doesn't matter. Almost as if it were designed that way? Now, why would they do that? That's an interesting question to ponder.

Xena taught me to honor and love the darkness in myself and others. Reclaiming that show taught me to identify the darkness as part of my gift of discernment and intuition. It was all part of the celestial plan.

Fig. 16. Gray, C. (2013). *Hope For the Sound Awakening.*[Red Digital Canvas Art]. Cameron Gray. https://cameron-gray.pixels.com/featured/hope-for-the-sound-awakening-cameron-gray.html.

CHAPTER 2

THE ADVANCED SHADOW WORK METHOD (ASWM)

Carl Jung's Quotes and Definition of Shadow

I want to begin by sharing with you how the Psychoanalyst Carl Jung, the creator of Shadow Work, described shadow in 1951[4]. "The shadow is a moral problem that challenges the whole ego-personality, for no one can become conscious of the shadow without considerable moral effort. To become conscious of it involves recognizing the dark aspects of the personality as present and real. This act is the essential condition for any kind of self-knowledge," (Jung, 1959).

He continues: "[Shadow is] those aspects of the personality that we choose to reject and repress. For one reason or another, we all have parts of ourselves that we don't like—or that we think society won't like—so we push those parts down into our unconscious psyches. It is this collection of repressed aspects of our identity that Jung referred to as our shadow self," (Jung, 1959). And finally: "We distance ourselves psychologically from those behaviors, emotions, and thoughts that we find dangerous," (Jung, 1959).

The Advanced Shadow Work Method

Are you feeling confused after reading that? All of Jung's work is a challenge to read through. I can understand it, but others who don't work in this profession have a hard time following. With shadow work's popularity increasing I felt compelled to honor his legendary insights in a digestible way. My approach adds modern discoveries and wisdom that speaks more fully to the spirit, which is living a human experience from a place of

---

[4] "Aion: Researches Into The Phenomenology Of The Self" wasn't published in America until 1959.

higher consciousness and feeling rather than a patriarchal and intellectualized place.

I realized that I see things differently from everyone else. I see shadow in every situation. It's hard for me *not* to see shadow. I already knew others didn't see what I saw in situations or what was underneath situations being described. It became clear as a mental health professional that I had a unique perspective and it differed drastically from other clinicians.

Call it a superpower or a gift, but I'm grateful to have this gift. The gift of seeing what's hidden underneath, the unconscious in situations, behaviors, thoughts, and actions. I see emotional needs, the shadow part of them, and someone's gifts and truth before they see it. I was blown away by what I had conscious awareness of. I had this gift for a reason.

My foundational skills are rooted in trauma therapy, and I'm very confident in my knowledge and experience in treating and healing trauma. At the same time, I also resented the limitations in so many areas when it came to this traditional approach to help clients heal and get where they want to be in their lives.

I learned many necessary skills during my time as a therapist: providing psychoeducation, like teaching people about their brain and nervous system connection, body feeling memory, and how trauma affects the whole system, including one's behavior. My experience as a therapist gave me wisdom to navigate and support lived emotional experiences, relational or attachment styles, coping and grounding skills, and communication skills around boundaries. There's so much about that profession I'm grateful for, because I use that wisdom all the time. Although I can't call myself a therapist anymore, I created my own kind of alternative therapy that instead offers well-rounded, holistic care for the mind, body, and soul.

THE ADVANCED SHADOW WORK METHOD

In the Advanced Shadow Work Method, or ASWM, whenever I'm meeting with clients for the first time I always ask the same questions: *What brought you to shadow work? Do you practice any coping and grounding skills?* If yes, I'll ask to hear more about what they do. This isn't a trick question, but I'm trying to help clients see the level of bias we all have about ourselves, and how frequently we lie or exaggerate to say we do something we don't. We do this to appear better and more responsible for ourselves than we are, which helps no one. This ingrained bias is a shadow program to reject our feelings and the emotions of others. This is why there's a mental health crisis.

The truth eventually rolls out—that clients don't always help themselves or know how. That's okay! When we can finally be honest about what we're doing and how we're feeling, we can take action. Otherwise, it's like being given the wrong address and not understanding why you can't find the fucking location. Without the correct address, you'll never arrive at your destination.

During the initial session, we'll discuss what issues they're having and what shadow work and digging they've done so far. We've all been conditioned or shadow programmed to be more comfortable and connected to an intellectual understanding versus emotional understanding. We're disconnected from ourselves due to the same patriarchal conditioning or shadow programming. We've literally been shadow programmed to reject, avoid, deny, and gaslight our emotional experience, our inner world, and that of others. When you're able to uncover the true reason why certain behaviors may be happening, that resonance will shift how you approach and understand yourself within the situation. You'll be able to give yourself more empathy.

Within this approach, I utilize many different concepts, including areas of research, insight from my own practice, trainings, certifications, degrees, initiations, clinical and magikal experiences, as well as my own lived experience. It all comes together to formulate my one-of-a-kind approach to shadow work. In truth, it's beyond shadow work, it's a form of healing that will have a positive, long-lasting impact on your life.

In ASWM, I'm not changing what Jung defined as shadow work per se, but I further explore the meaning through realms he never considered 100 years ago when he first created the theory.

I agree with most of how Jung describes shadow, but it's not just a shadow self and it doesn't need to be fixed and changed. It's technically shadow selves, as in plural, and we don't use rigid, abusive patriarchal words to describe the shadow selves like fixed, changed, irregular, irrational, shameful, negative, bad, etc. He thinks that these shadow parts have been rejected by you and others. That's true, to a point, but there are some shadows that you wouldn't even know about or consider, because they don't come from this life or originate with you. It's an unhealed emotional wound that has been passed down ancestrally as heart disease or low self-worth.

In ASWM, the term "shadow" is used to identify the shadow parts of you, but it also refers to your subconscious and unconscious mind in general. Anything that's not in your conscious mind is in shadow. If it's hidden out of awareness, it's in the darkness. It's in shadow. That's why we don't have conscious access to our shadows, they can't be accessed consciously. You must enter into an altered state of consciousness to ascertain certain memories and shadows, some of which are hidden so deep you'd be clueless about them otherwise.

Shadow work extends to generational, ancestral, past lives, and collective trauma that has, over time, displayed as behaviors that affect your life or act as blocks to achieving your desires. It's a choice to take on the responsibility of healing and removing that block from your bloodline.

For bigger themes found within collective trauma, we tend to be able to guess what the narrative and shadows are, and why they're there. Therefore, we can guess what self-talk to use, what grounding skills are needed, and work to reprogram new thoughts and behaviors to support the healing and removal. The goal is to free you from collective trauma.

Recent neuroscience and brain scan studies theorize the levels of access and utilization of our consciousness and brain activity that we have at any given moment: we only have access to five to ten percent of our conscious awareness at all times. 50 to 60 percent is subconscious, and 30-40% is unconscious. Theoretically, within this approach we're living 90-95% of our daily waking lives in shadow—choosing, doing, thinking, acting, and behaving from shadow.

Once I help people see their shadow in the situation, I provide a guided meditation to meet with the shadow parts that are currently upset and creating problems, or that need the most help right now. Every meditation is unique and tailored to each client and their shadow, because we're having a direct conversation with that part of you.

I ask questions of your shadow and we get real-time answers about what's going on, why they're showing up, causing chaos, and what they need to feel safe, ultimately creating a more stable climate for you and your shadows. Then, an agreement is made about the behaviors, self-talk statements, actions and frequency of how often they want you to meet with them to heal the relationship.

The table below shows why I chose to use guided meditation with clients. It takes them into an Alpha wave state between 8-12 Hz which is used for optimal super learning. The Alpha brain wave state "bridges the conscious to the subconscious and is derived from white matter in the brain. White matter is the part of the brain that connects all the parts with each other," (The Science of Brainwaves, 2024). In this state, "you may feel relaxed, not agitated, not drowsy, tranquil, and conscious. The way you get there is through meditation or in-action (no action, just being or mindfulness). Physiologically it promotes healing and relaxation. 8-10 Hz creates balance, inner-awareness of self, mind, and body integration," (The Science of Brainwaves, 2024). Just above that, "10-12 Hz creates centering, healing, and mind/body connection," (The Science of Brainwaves, 2024).

Coming out of a mild meditative state, clients then enter into a Gamma wave state, between 30-44 Hz, which promotes feeling more connected with themselves and consciousness, with higher levels of understanding and perception of themselves and the work, solidifying the experience further. "In this state, you may feel alert or agitated doing tasks like mental activity i.e. math or planning. It connects with the physiological activation of the mind and body functions. You will become more alert but it can produce agitation," (The Science of Brainwaves, 2024). This state allows you to wield elemental fire energy, which is forward motion and can be challenging. This is where clients can get out of balance during shadow work. Imbalances are often caused by staying in masculine energy for too long to try to get things done, but it's important to remember to tend to your emotional experience after shadow work.

We've been shadow programmed and conditioned to think we want to always be in forward motion, completing and reaching goals in order to feel self-worth. That productivity-focused energy can quickly become toxic masculinity if you're not careful. It's important to take the time to integrate lessons, slow down, and meditate on them. If not, you'll burn out during your self-healing work and skip over a bunch of lessons that you'll have to repeat again until you actually learn them.

During and after meditation, I see clients transition to an Epsilon wave (below 0.5 Hz) where they feel spiritually connected to themselves, as if they just had an out-of-body or mystical experience. They feel inspired and are conscious of what they need to do moving forward to heal. It's an extremely powerful state.

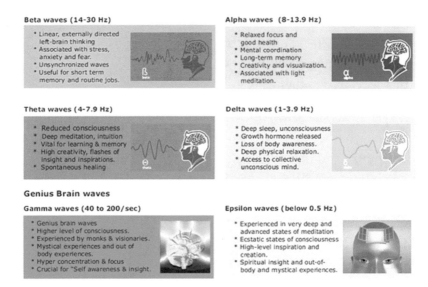

Fig. 17. [Chart of Brainwave States]. (n.d.). Brain Training Centre. https://www.braintrainingcentre.com.au/brain-waves

Guided meditation is the key that gives clients access to feeling empathy for themselves for the first time. Seeing themselves, and hearing how their self-talk is impacting their younger self is what hits differently. What changes people's view about self-talk is realizing the weight and power of their words, and understanding this practice is having a direct impact on their entire existence.

Typically, we only meet with a shadow one time in meditation. All of the work comes after. That's why this is a lifelong journey. You can get the answers, but it doesn't mean your life changes when you receive them and it immediately makes everything better. Clients typically know the answers already, they just don't want to believe them or see them, or don't want to put in the work. Many think it can't be that simple.

After the meditation, we take time to discuss your experience and what you learned, what you're going to do, and how you're going to get there based on what the shadow told us. We focus heavily on self-talk and reprogramming thoughts to match the new energy and emotional experience a client wants to have and that feels true to them.

The real shadow work is related to how you support yourself in the journey of self-exploration and discovery, how you empathize and meet yourself with compassion and patience, and how you work diligently to feel your emotions. It's a process of breaking old patterns without numbing out, and without avoiding, denying, rejecting, or suppressing. Real change comes with feeling these emotions and releasing them. It involves practicing coping and grounding skills daily, practicing healthy, loving self-talk, and creating healthy boundaries for optimal growth and well-being.

I don't have a straightforward methodology that I use with every client. That may be why it was so difficult for me to wrap my head around how I could explain this method to people so they understand it, but also hold space for something that's free-flowing and uniquely tailored to each person.

I train people how to see shadows in their life, body, emotions, and behaviors. I teach coping and grounding skills, encouraging each person to practice them habitually to support their emotional regulation journey, because that's what leads to true wealth, safety, and quality of life. I teach how to establish self-talk in a way that resonates and makes a difference, and that works long-term. I teach people how to forgive and love themselves anyway, while also having those hard conversations with their shadows to address why they haven't been showing up for themselves. I teach people how to repair their relationship with themselves. I help people understand how to continue working with their shadows.

I advise clients on when to come back for another session, or when they need to see a specific healer to access the memories and expansion they can't access on their own. I teach people how to release their wounds by seeing the truth of their emotions, to analyze their behavior in order to understand what emotional needs aren't being met. I teach clients how to be true self-healers, to use these skills to heal and perceive in a way that activates an alchemical release altering their reality. I teach people how to lean into their whimsical experience by incorporating magik in small ways to co-create an abundant, beautiful life without all the extra baggage and boring conformity.

Over time, you'll become an expert in your shadow work. You'll master how to show up for yourself by navigating your shadows, and do so with greater and greater ease, because you have the skills to do so. You'll be so impressed by how much easier it is for you to identify shadows everywhere, which will help you trust yourself more. Trusting and listening to your intuition heightens your power of discernment. That means you won't get fooled easily, and you'll see the truth in situations others don't. It's like you're two steps ahead of your environment. Your shadow work will impact others in your life. You'll want to foster the relationships that support this growth, and who are inspired by you. Those who don't support your growth will leave your life. That's the balance, the scales of the Universe, always pushing out what no longer matches your vibration.

I also use the term previously discussed, shadow program, to describe collective, generational, ancestral, and past life traumas that just about every person on the planet has. These stem from oppression, abandonment, neglect, shame, guilt, low self-worth, grief, fear of loss, and disempowerment. If we can't find these themes in your current life, and your shadow hasn't started shifting or improving, then we can assume it comes from that deeper source. There are times when we can access the past selves through shadow work meditation and I can lead clients in ancestral guided meditation to receive information about what healing needs to take place.

When it's a deeply generalized collective emotional experience, we can still do the shadow work meditation because your shadow parts will tell you what you need to heal to release this story from your being. We don't have to enter meditation each time to begin reprogramming and releasing narratives that have been conditioned into our systems over centuries and lifetimes.

Often, the block that's felt is not the answer you typically think it is, because it's a story or narrative that doesn't align with you in this life. It's not your story at all. That's why it's interfering with your unique vibrational signature, because it's a hidden shadow programmed narrative playing in the background without your conscious awareness. And it's *absolutely* working against you and blocking the things you want from coming into your life. Only when you enter full alignment energetically with your deepest desires will the Universe provide you with what you want. It's like a magnet, or law of attraction, it's manifestation magik.

Therefore, self-talk and reprogramming your thoughts and perceptions is the biggest chunk of work. The work is to become aware of all of the narratives and feelings as they happen, and work to address them, and integrate these changes in a loving and empathetic way (that last part is the hardest part for most people).

The most difficult aspect of this process is self-talk. Which makes a lot of sense, because 95% of the things we say to ourselves go unnoticed since we're so used to hearing them. (A loving reminder that we only have access to five to ten percent of our conscious awareness at all times.) It's like that low-level hum of a fan in the background that disappears because it's so familiar. People are so used to speaking and relating to themselves in a certain way, and seeing or believing themselves to be a certain way, that it takes a bit of time to process and believe that the negative thoughts you hold about yourself aren't actually true and never came from you in the first place.

We're much tougher on ourselves than other people, and that's due to the shadow programming and conditioning from society, which includes over thousands of years of oppression, abuse, mistreatment, diminishing of our sense of selves, and disconnection from Mother Earth and all of her children— including each other. Self-talk is all about returning back to the heart space. It's about creating the safety to say and feel the things that are *true*.

Society and consumerism tell us we're not good enough. Shadow programming is what makes us think we're too old or too fat, or that we need this or that to be okay. Consumerism trains us to buy products or use objects that are full of chemicals and poison. Yet, people eat it the fuck up and do whatever the mainstream tells them to do. It's horrifying. Contemporary society in the West is built on the sick model, not the preventative model. Let's begin to see ourselves as starting from scratch with our self-talk. Start over with yourself. Form a new way of relating to yourself, try seeing and thinking of yourself in a different light. This all takes time, and there will always be a lot of shadows, narratives, and beliefs that will try to validate the old patterns and ways of being. The key to noticing when your self-talk is unhelpful is that your emotions and feelings in your body become tense and intense. Feeling unpleasant physical sensations in your body is the signal your self-talk is off and that you need to pay more attention.

Shadow work can be an isolating experience, and it's meant to be, at times, while doing this deep inner work and introspection. But it's also important to have connections that help support you. Learning how to successfully communicate your shadow work, emotions, expectations, needs, and boundaries in your respective relationships helps set you up for continued progress and building a new conscious program on your journey. This will provide you with the skills of empowerment and the ability to protect your healing journey in this sacred work with the utmost integrity and balance. Set yourself up for success by learning the language of your mind, body, soul, and spirit so you can create a life that reflects and is aligned with both who you are now and who you are becoming.

The coming chapters go into greater detail about each step of the Advanced Shadow Work Method. If you plan to practice the method on your own, taking notes will be helpful.

CHAPTER 3

WHAT IS TRAUMA?

In my approach, I theorize that shadow only exists because of trauma. There are few exceptions when shadow isn't a result of trauma, including all of the unconscious body processes, spiritual and higher conscious information, passive information you're absorbing all the time through technology, ethereal beings, and the energy and thoughts of all sentient beings around you. You're also not consciously aware of them because they're existing outside of your conscious awareness until you become conscious of them. Trauma is the result of exposure to an incident or series of events that are emotionally disturbing or life-threatening, and that have lasting adverse effects on the individual's functioning, mental, physical, social, emotional, and spiritual well-being. Your caretakers, parents, or environment should provide the needed skills to help make sense of what happened, to nurture and soothe our nervous system, and to help us feel loved and safe after. But that doesn't always happen.

Trauma is the result when we're left to make up the meanings ourselves. You narrate who you are, who others are in relation to you, and your environment through that lens of lack of safety or danger. You can easily narrate the world as against you, that it's your fault bad things happened, and it's something about who you are at your core that's wrong, broken, or unlovable. The story created, the meaning made from it, and how we were not supported or cared for creates how you relate to others, connect, attach, and establish beliefs, all of which can be shaped around one traumatic experience.

Trauma can happen to anyone at any age and has happened to everyone. Not a single person on this planet is without trauma. American culture often espouses a preconceived notion of what trauma is—that it's this horrible, drastic, Earth-shattering event like living in a war zone or your best friend being murdered. That couldn't be further from the truth. Trauma is anything that dysregulates your nervous system without the proper tools and support to make helpful and healing meaning about what you just experienced. One can feel trauma every time he or she feels disappointment, because caregivers never taught him or her how to make sense of disappointment or self-soothe when feeling that way. Therefore, disappointment can feel like despair, or like your whole world is ending every time, which is very traumatic. Trauma can be breakups or separations of any kind, moving from your hometown, getting arrested, family or friends passing, or your animal guardian passing, getting outed, bullying, not having your feelings cared about or validated, and not feeling like you have a voice. This also includes physical trauma or injury, as that's programmed in your body the same way as emotional trauma.

Even if you don't think you've experienced trauma in this life, you did before this life, and so did your ancestors. No matter what, you will feel these emotions play out as your own without a clue that the pain you're experiencing may not even stem from your own life.

We all have generational, ancestral, collective, and past life trauma with unanimous themes of oppression, abuse, corruption, violation, and being taken advantage of in some way. These traumas work through shadow to keep us in a state of subservience, staying asleep and unconscious, and having low self-worth and low self-love. This is so we wouldn't want more for ourselves or know that more is possible. We would never know our worth, or know that we're worthy of everything we desire. In past lives if we weren't oppressed, then we were the oppressor in power. No matter what, you will experience all sides of a situation in different lives as repeated lessons continue to pop up in your current life. That's the balance or karmic cycle and pattern, it's how we complete soul contracts by learning and completing the lessons on all sides of the situation.

We're easier to control as a collective when we're barely keeping our heads above water, beaten down within the patriarchal paradigms and systems that create fear, stress, trauma, burnout, disease, greed, vanity, materialism, consumerism, scarcity, productivity, toxic masculine energy, wounded feminine energy, and anxiety[5].

Your shadows are brilliant. They know if they act out they could get your attention, and you might listen and notice them rather than deny or reject them. That's the only way you would ever know they existed. They become your grateful guide and road map to point out exactly what you need to heal and how to help yourself if you choose to honor them and listen.

Traumatic events have been shown to damage the rational thinking mind: the hippocampus, amygdala, and prefrontal cortex which deal with our memory, emotional regulation, and decision-making. This makes it harder to heal trauma because of the impact it has on a subconscious level, leaving individuals with memory symptoms like ADHD/ADD or dissociation (not remembering the event), and an inability to regulate emotional experience, which precipitates making decisions from shadow or indecisiveness due to confusion and lack of trust in yourself to make correct choices.

In this holistic approach to healing trauma, the theory is that ancestral, generational, past life, and collective trauma are passed

---

[5] For definitions of both toxic masculine energy and wounded feminine energy see the glossary in the front of the book.

down through bloodlines, as blood (water) holds memory, aka your DNA is coded memory. It's also recorded in your unconscious mind and your body feeling memory—because the experiences went unhealed, or were repressed, suppressed, avoided, and denied. Therefore, unhealed trauma gets passed down as a shadow program hidden in and dictating your emotions, behaviors, and beliefs without you having any conscious awareness that it doesn't originate from you.

When it comes to physical illnesses in the body, especially when it's genetic, I theorize these are related to ancestral trauma that's been passed down. My hypothesis is the emotional energy manifests into an object of disease that's concentrated in the body where the trauma was originally stored. Science and genetics understand this as genetic markers of predisposition to genetic traits that could be expressed and activated or are inactive and dormant. This leads to some family members experiencing the disease and other family members only displaying the genetic markers while the disease itself remains dormant.

Research into the link between trauma and disease is improving, but it's still hard to scientifically prove. Many mental health professionals and scientists are aware that we've been missing a huge piece of the puzzle regarding the skyrocketing mental and physical health crises our society has been experiencing over the last century. More and more studies are being released that indicate a clear link between health issues and the deep emotional trauma of catastrophic events like wars, family violence, and brutal colonization that's passed down through generations, and we're slowly but surely adding evidence to this theory.

As a Reiki Master and energetic healer, I can attest that trauma and emotions get stored in the body as energy. When they're repressed, ignored, avoided, or denied with each generation, they grow and manifest as physical illnesses in the body. The table below shows the Root Chakra system along with characteristics of expression, connected organs, how they're affected, signs and symptoms, and how to heal or improve the chakra and the organ functioning.

The Primary Chakra Characteristics

Chakra	Organs and Glands	Physical Imbalances	Personal Traits	Emotional and Mental Imbalances
1st: Root Color: Red	Blood Spine Nervous System Bladder Male Reproductive Vagina Tailbone Sacrum	Anemia; Lack of Energy Flu-Viral Infections Low Blood Pressure Bladder Infections Sluggish Digestion Bone Marrow Disorder Poor Circulation Impotence or Frigidity Male Infertility Sciatica Lower Sacrum Pain Varicose Veins Low Immune System Rectal Disorders Rectal Cancers Leukemia	Family Identity Group safety & Security Physical Survival Needs Ability to stand up for self Feeling at home with life Being present in life Social & Family order Connection with Earth Physical energy/vitality Physical manifestation Life force on Earth Male Sexuality	Depression & Hopelessness Spaced out Disconnection from life Money/abundance issues Fears regarding safety or security Egotistical Domineering or Dominated Lack of confidence Can't achieve goals Self-destructive or suicidal Fear of abandonment Preoccupation with material things Isolation & loneliness Fear of change
2nd: Sacral	Skin	Kidney problems	Control over self &	Repression/Inhibition

Fig. 9. *The Primary Chakra Characteristics.* Usui Reiki Level 1 Class Manual. Raven Moon Healing Arts, 2022.

Trauma is continually passed down until someone discovers these generational, ancestral, collective, and past life wounds need to be healed through shadow work and taking a holistic approach to healing your physical body. Healing various traumas will heal the linked physical illness or ailment where it was stored, especially if you have added to it in this life.

Epigenetics is the biological study of inherited traits. It explores how our behavior and environment can change how our genes work, by changing how the body reads the genetic sequence. "In epigenetics, generational trauma manifests in offspring as an increased risk for PTSD, anxiety, obesity, and diabetes," (Yehuda & Lehrner, 2018). Whatever narratives and past trauma you inherited—or are coming into this current life with—all of it will impact every other part of your life, and will likely be expressed differently by each of your family members.

Dr. Lipton, a cell biologist known for trying to bridge the gap between spirit and science says, "Over 90 percent of disease is a total reflection of the environment and especially our programming: the disempowering, self-sabotaging behaviors that we acquired in the first seven years. Since those disempowering programs are based on our environment and perception, and since we can change the environment and our perception, we have the power to free ourselves from disease and to start living that happily-ever-after honeymoon of life experiences that we all believe that we can have. The way we do that is by eliminating the self-sabotaging subconscious programs acquired during the first seven years of our lives," (Gustafson, 2017).

Dr. Lipton continues, "A change in perception of an individual can change their biology, virtually immediately. Studies showed the genetic readout of some inflammatory genes in a group of people who meditated for eight hours, the activity of the genes changed in less than eight hours. You can change your genetic activity by how you change your response to the environment. The blueprint of your life is based on perception because your genes will change according to your perception via epigenetics. The emphasis is fully turned around to recognize our perceptions, via signal transduction, are translated into biological behavior. These factors control your behavior, but also your genetic activity," (Gustafson, 2017). This shows you the incredible potential we have to heal ourselves and change our DNA. We can change the physical body with our perception.

Don't you wonder why this isn't common knowledge? Think about how many systems in our society profit off our illness, disease, poor mental health, and unconscious behaviors. Time to wake the fuck up people and think for yourself. Believe that you are magik and Source. You are consciousness itself. You can transform your whole existence.

Trauma can be difficult to pinpoint for someone whose past emotional experiences were denied or not supported as a child. This creates a lack of understanding about emotions and emotional experiences. I'm sorry if that was your experience. It's okay if the above is true and an individual has been stuck in the on or off state. When paralyzed in this way, the best thing you can do for yourself is to admit it aloud to yourself. Then say, "but I love and accept myself anyway." It may sound like, "I've been stuck in the off position without knowing it for ten years, but I love and accept myself anyway." You might laugh a little, that's good.

The real key, if you're stuck, is to practice coping and grounding skills until you're blue in the face. Practice the techniques when you're calm, nothing is wrong, or you're just a little upset, bored, sad, mad—literally do it for everything *daily*. This is the most important life skill I can impart to anyone. Grounding is the greatest gift you can give yourself.

I've been selected by Spirit to help assist and empower the collective to live beyond their trauma, beyond life as a trauma survivor. This doesn't diminish or erase how it impacted who you are and who you have become. You wouldn't be you without it. You gained wisdom and lessons from that experience, that's why it happened. Sometimes, trauma happens to clear our karmic contracts. We've forgotten the true purpose trauma brings us: we wouldn't know or see the light without darkness. We need it to transform and grow into higher conscious beings. Without that truth, we become disconnected from our higher wisdom and go into blame or victimization mode, pulling our whole world and perception into shadowed darkness. We were never meant to hold onto the trauma as a badge of honor. It's only because those in power have kept us from the knowledge of how to heal. By removing these blocks we remember we can heal ourselves, hold the power to change in our genetics, and that it's possible to release trauma from our being entirely.

We're encouraged to approach this from a functional perspective rather than an emotionally sensitive one. One factor is related to our shadow's storage space. It's necessary to clean up our storage space because of the timeline we're entering, the Age of Aquarius is breathing elements of fire and air into our lives. It's fast-moving, fast-paced energy that's all about the mind (air) and taking action (fire), as well as manifesting and creating (air and fire) things into being through the power of the mind (air). We will be able to manifest at incredible speeds. We need to be extremely mindful and careful of how and what we think about because we will create it. You will not forget the trauma that happened, it's a part of what has forced you to transform, but it has also transformed you.

You are now free of the limitations, holds, patterns, emotions, and beliefs as they will be completely programmed out of your being. When you heal, a new version of you is created in its place that no longer has that trauma. The only thing that keeps trauma alive and affecting your life are the shadow thoughts repeating the same cycles and experiences that no longer exist. The shadow thoughts keep reinforcing the past trauma as a current lived experience and reality. That's right, you only continue to experience the symptoms of trauma because your thoughts and perception make it so, not because it's still affecting you.

When we fixate on experiences or symptoms, everything fades to shadow and the trauma continues to take up sacred real estate. While you aren't forgetting the wisdom of what happened to you, you're no longer emotionally impacted in the same low vibrational way. You have alchemized your trauma into something new that serves your highest good and the highest good of all. You might feel gratitude, forgiveness, and love now instead of hate and rage. Sometimes, it's hard to let that identity or mindset go because of how deeply it's embedded into our subconscious shadow programming. It brings up big emotions and internal reactions, which then need to be healed and released through shadow work.

I created a daily check-in list for clients to learn about themselves and better navigate their day according to their needs. I hope you find as much value in it as they have. For those interested, I've included a **QR** code under the Resources section of this book to access the daily check-ins as a free PDF that you can download from my website.

Tips to Healing Your Trauma With the ASWM

1. You have to feel it to heal it. You must feel the emotion to release the trauma and move past it. Being cerebral and staying intellectual will only cause you to feel stuck for a frustrating amount of time. A purely intellectual examination of your trauma without experiencing the accompanying emotions results in an unsatisfactory, anticlimactic answer and unfulfilling experience. From there, you will have to go to drastic or radical measures to bypass the cognitive straitjacket on your emotions and to tap into feeling them to release them.

2. All trauma is unique. Don't compare your struggles to an experience that someone else might be having. Trauma isn't a competition to see who's more traumatized than the other, or who has

the most wrong with them. We can relate and share experiences, but always state: "My experience is nothing like yours." You don't want to diminish or devalue your own or other's experiences and feelings. Refrain from trauma dumping without asking first. Not everyone wants to hear about your trauma or has the bandwidth to handle what it could trigger in them.

3. You will learn during your trauma healing journey that what you need most is often the thing you most actively avoid and deny. Trust is a huge piece. Trust the journey. Despite understanding that conquering this thing will level up your healing game, and propel you to the next seemingly insurmountable chapter, you might find yourself avoiding healing that wound at every turn. For some absurd reason, we want to deny ourselves this peace, or reject a certain reality because it doesn't fit into the narrative we envisioned for ourselves, or it isn't what we were programmed to believe we want.

4. Take breaks. Don't do trauma work constantly. You must recover from healing wounds and doing the deep work. It's hard work sitting with uncomfortability and building awareness. Being more conscious is exhausting. It takes a lot of energy to use more conscious brain activity. You need rest and relaxation as part of healing your nervous system and to allow integration. Slowing down whenever you have the opportunity makes a world of difference. Also, remember to bring in spontaneity; if you've been doing shadow work in isolation a lot, mix it up and go to a show, go dancing, or hang out with your friends. Every now and then you need human connection, touch, serotonin, smiles, laughter, to skip doing shadow work for a night, not look at your trauma, not look at yourself and this work like a project, and to leave your home and the Underworld.

5. Try not to get stuck in your trauma and overidentify with it. When it becomes your narrative and story it energetically

intertwines into the fabric of your reality, because life is still felt and spoken into it. If you do this, you will manifest it over and over again into your reality.

6. Hear this loudly—*please do not* do trauma work without practicing coping and grounding skills *first*. Getting those skills in place is like going through a safety course for a dangerous but life-changing activity like jumping out of a plane. You definitely want to do the class, pay attention, and practice, because what you learned may very well save your life. You might think it's silly to compare the importance of attending your skydiving safety class to learning coping and grounding skills, but I honestly believe if you practice grounding and coping skills enough, and integrate them into your daily routine, they will save your life in more ways than one. Not only will they save your mental health, but your physical and spiritual health as well. The more grounded and calm you are, the healthier and more youthful you will be. These skills will help you maintain emotional balance, gain emotional intelligence, have healthier relationships, look more youthful and beautiful, and even help you stay more fit. Your shadows will trust you because you're helping them and keeping them safe, and therefore, building trust with yourself. You will become happier and start making better choices for yourself as positive consequences.

Examples of Ways We Experience Trauma and Shadow

- **An example of trauma getting passed down in a family and expressed differently through individual sisters.** You and your sibling experience the same emotional abuse and trauma from a parent who would body shame and food shame. Each sibling experiencing the same situation had vastly different perspectives, emotions, internalizations, self-esteem, self-worth, and relational patterns they created out of that trauma. Both sisters experienced varying levels of body issues, body dysmorphia, low self-worth, poor self-talk, and disordered eating. One sibling is more anxious as an adult, has trouble eating, is very critical of herself and others, and has a small circle of friends. The other sibling as an adult is more "chill" but is really dissociated and checked out, overeats, doesn't have boundaries, and has a large circle of friends. When you're in shadow functioning from those wounds, you're not consciously choosing what you're doing, your trauma is. When you choose to become aware and more conscious in every aspect of your life, you see how much power you wield through your thoughts shaping every second.

- **Examples of ways we actively deny or avoid the answer:** One example of this includes avoiding positive or loving self-talk. Others are avoiding empathy with self or others, avoiding meditation, and avoiding using grounding skills. Also, not ending that habit or behavior that's not aligned with your highest self and true values or behavior that lowers your vibration when you want to resonate higher. It can be not ending that relationship you know is toxic, that your shadow tells you to stay in even though you wonder deep down if your whole future begins after this person finally leaves your life. Sometimes, it's our addictions, that thing we don't want to let go of and want to keep pretending is going to be fine, when we know deep down what we truly seek is on the other side. Maybe it's leaving the job that pays you a ridiculous amount of money but is soul-sucking work. Maybe you feel like you work for the devil and hate your job. That hate bleeds into your life painting it all red. A levee must break, either way, and the Universe will give you repeated patterns and situations until you align with your highest truth and commit.

CHAPTER 4

BRIEF PSYCHOEDUCATION FOR GOOD MEASURE

As a mental health practitioner and former therapist who has a decade of trauma-informed clinical experience under my belt, I've learned how important it is for clients to be informed. This includes being informed about what happens in their body, brain, nervous system, behaviors, and ways of relating that are affected by trauma. I've seen the level of empowerment it brings my clients when they fully understand why X, Y, and Z happen. I theorize this is meaningful to us because historically people in positions of power didn't explain things to us in a way we could understand. It's especially meaningful when that information is about what's happening below the surface in your emotional life. When individuals can better understand what's happening internally on a tangible physical level, it cuts them a little slack. There are a lot of people usually in need of a little slack to help alleviate the stubborn "tough love" shadow program we've been conditioned to believe is what motivates us, or we'd never get anything done without it.

For those of you who are unfamiliar with what psychoeducation is, it refers to "providing clear information to patients and their families about mental health conditions, to improve understanding, support and treatment outcomes," (Herrera et al., 2023).

THE NERVOUS SYSTEM (NS)- 2 MAIN SYSTEMATIC PARTS: THE CENTRAL NERVOUS SYSTEM (CNS) & PERIPHERAL NERVOUS SYSTEM (PNS)

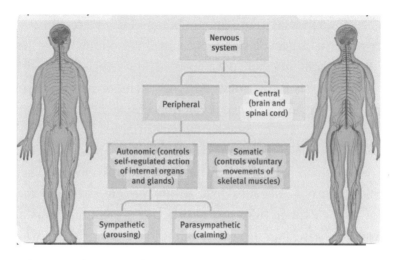

Fig. 1 "The Functional Divisions of the Human Nervous System." *The Nervous System.* 5 March 2024, http://digfir-published.macmillanusa.com/pel3e/pel3e_ch2_4.html.

The Central Nervous System (CNS)

Your central nervous system, or your body's command center, is made up of two parts—the brain and spinal cord.

Nerves connect the two parts: the brain and spinal cord. Nerves carry electrical signals from your brain to other parts of your body (feeling heat or pain). The CNS basically coordinates everything that your body does.

Neurons

Neurons are special cells that carry your nerve's electrical signals like very fragile wires connecting your brain to different parts of your body to tell them what to do (move your arm).

There are two types of neurons: sensory and motor neurons. Sensory neurons are constantly scanning your environment picking up information to send to your brain about what is happening around you (A lion is coming! You better fucking run!).

Motor neurons carry instructions down from your brain to your specific body parts so you can react appropriately (The brain sends a signal to legs—move your legs, run bitch or you'll die, there's a lion!).

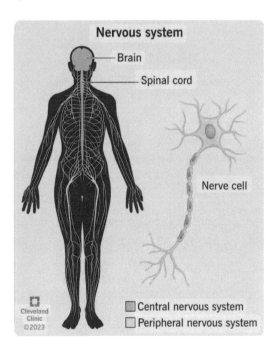

Fig. 2. *"Nervous System."* 2023. *Cleveland Clinic,* https://my.clevelandclinic.org/health/body/21202-nervous-system.

Window of Tolerance—Stress vs. Trauma

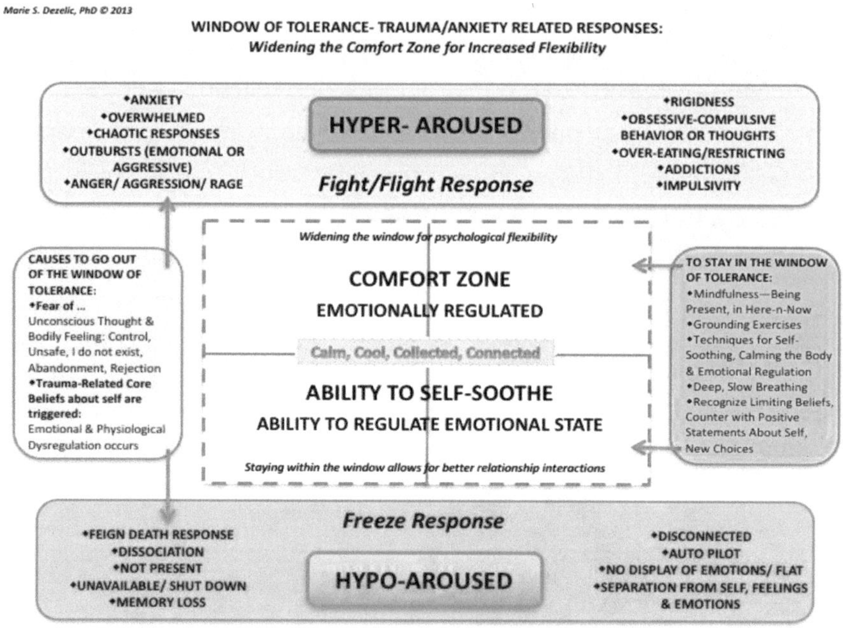

Marie S. Dezelic, PhD © 2013

WINDOW OF TOLERANCE- TRAUMA/ANXIETY RELATED RESPONSES:
Widening the Comfort Zone for Increased Flexibility

Fig. 3. Dezelic, Marie. "Window of Tolerance—Trauma/Anxiety Related Responses: Widening the Comfort Zone for Increased Flexibility." 2013. *Downloadable Handouts: Choices for Self-Help and Transformation.* 3 May 2024, https://www.drmariedezelic.com/window-of-tolerance--traumaanxiety-rela.

In periods of stress, the body's four F's: flight, fight, freeze, or fawn response activate and a normally regulated nervous system can experience stress and then return to baseline (calm) when the potential threat is over. The period where you can self-regulate is called the window of tolerance. Most people move through several of these cycles daily. My clients have heard me say this many times: we're always actively trying to build a window of tolerance where they've never had one by practicing grounding and coping skills, using supportive self-talk, and mindfulness.

However, the whole system and window of tolerance work very differently when the body experiences trauma rather than smaller stressful situations. Traumatic events push the nervous system outside of its ability to regulate or activate your parasympathetic nervous system itself. This means experiencing swings of highs and lows. In this situation, the nervous system becomes conditioned to exist in a state of fear. This state continues into adulthood and is triggered by things that might seem unrelated to a person's childhood trauma. For example, a man who grew up in a war zone might have a trauma response to the backfiring of a car exhaust like it's a gun firing. The nervous system and body are ready to respond in fight-or-flight, and are stuck in a hypervigilant state due to long-term exposure to trauma, also known as C-PTSD or complex trauma, and healing is more complicated after being stuck in hypo or hyperactivation for a long time. There's unraveling and rebuilding that has to take place (Understanding Trauma, 2023).

To better understand the window of tolerance, consider the following examples. You reach for the almond milk, but realize there's not enough left for your breakfast. You stress out and get a little flustered as you figure out a new meal plan, but once you figure it out, you calm back down and start making your new meal. Another example is thinking you're going to be late to work, but you arrive five minutes early and let out a big sigh, calming down quickly and maybe even laughing it off. Finally, say you get a stressful email at work with a task to complete immediately. You complete the task and everything is fine, but you had a surge of anxiety and stress when the notification popped up on your screen that sent you into panic mode. Once the task was complete, you released a big sigh activating your vagus nerve and telling your nervous system it's safe now. You return back to baseline.

THE PERIPHERAL NERVOUS SYSTEM (PNS) IS SUBDIVIDED INTO: THE AUTONOMIC NERVOUS SYSTEM (ANS) AND THE SOMATIC NERVOUS SYSTEM (SNS)

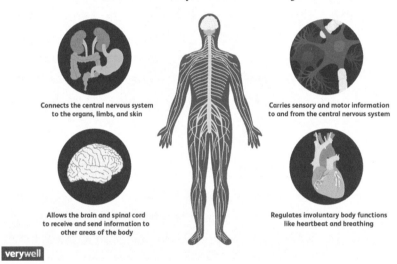

Fig. 4. Cherry, Kendra. "How the Peripheral Nervous System Works." *VeryWellMind,* https://www.verywellmind.com/what-is-the-peripheral-nervous-system-2795465. Accessed 3 May 2024.

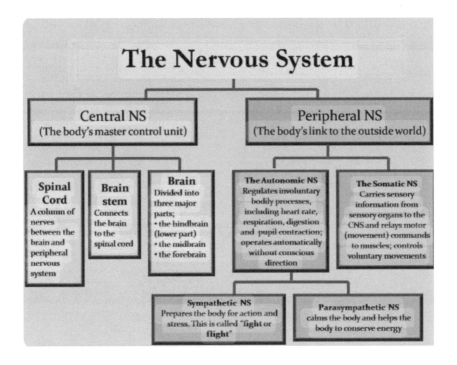

Fig. 5. Geara, R. [Rolla]. (n.d.). *Nervous System and Sense Organs* [Pinterest post]. Pinterest. Retrieved May 17, 2024. https://pin.it/4ZsVt7dwG

Both the Autonomic Nervous System (ANS) and Somatic Nervous System (SNS) are motor systems that regulate the activity of muscle fibers or secretory cells, which release useful substances like hormones, enzymes, lubrication, and sweat. Your SNS involves things you can consciously sense and do. The SNS includes all the nerves that run to and from the spinal cord and send information to and from the muscles and senses. Somatic nerves always activate the contraction of the somatic muscles, while ANS fibers will either activate or inhibit the vital organs. Your ANS works without you thinking about it, running behind-the-scenes processes that keep you alive (Akinrodoye & Lui, 2022). Think of the ANS as automatic instead of autonomic—it's your autopilot and requires zero conscious thought. It's second nature.

AUTONOMIC NERVOUS SYSTEM (ANS) HOUSES TWO MAIN DIVISIONS: SYMPATHETIC NERVOUS SYSTEM (SNS) AND THE PARASYMPATHETIC NERVOUS SYSTEM (PNS)

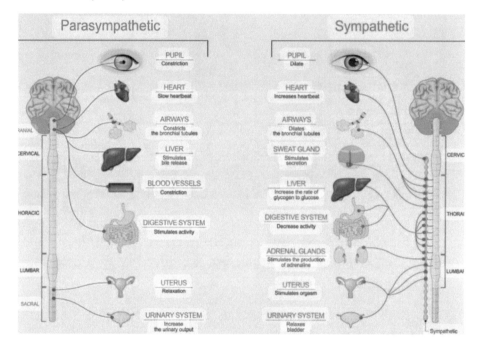

Fig. 6. Salim, Roxanna, "An Introduction to the Sympathetic and Parasympathetic Nervous System." 2019. *Imotions* https://imotions.com/blog/learning/research-fundamentals/nervous-system/

The Sympathetic Nervous System (SNS)

Trauma has a significant impact on the SNS, which is responsible for our fight-or-flight response. When an individual has experienced trauma, the SNS is activated, releasing the stress hormones cortisol and adrenaline. These hormones increase your heart rate, blood pressure, and respiratory rate in preparation for the body to survive a perceived threat.

When a person experiences trauma over an extended period of time "some individual's systems can get stuck in the 'on' position, or fight, flight, or fawn, being overstimulated and unable to calm down when trauma is ongoing or repeated. Experiencing anxiety, hypervigilance, difficulty sleeping (insomnia or nightmares), anger, irritability, restlessness, panic, and hyperactivity can all result when you stay in the ready-to-react mode. This physical state of hyperarousal is stressful for every organ and system in the body, leading to chronic stress," (Understanding Trauma, 2023).

The Parasympathetic Nervous System (PNS)

Trauma impacts the PNS's role which is responsible for rest and relaxation. We're not born with a PNS. The PNS is grown over time through mirroring with a grounded nervous system via skin-to-skin contact as an infant and developed as we grow older. One of my graduate school professors explained it like this—if the SNS is the gas, the PNS is the brakes. It's what helps you have a window of tolerance and what you activate in order to gain a window of tolerance. The PNS is why you can relax or be calm, and the SNS is why you can run from someone attacking you or fight back. You need both.

Chronic activation of the SNS can interfere with the PNS's ability to restore the body to a calm state of balance. For other individuals, their nervous system is stuck in the "off" position. Their survival response is to shut down and they're unable to connect with their body, they're dissociated in the frozen survival response which can result in depression, disconnection, fatigue, and lethargy, (Understanding Trauma, 2023).

The Vagus Nerve

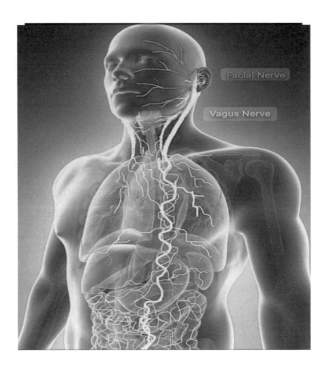

Fig. 7. Kenny, B. J., & Bordoni, B. "Neuroanatomy, Cranial Nerve 10 (Vagus Nerve)." *National Library of Medicine: National Center for Biotechnology Information* [Internet]. StatPearls Publishing. 2022 Nov 7, https://www.ncbi.nlm.nih.gov/books/NBK537171/?report=reader#!po=81.2500. Accessed 4 May 2024.

I introduce the vagus nerve because it's largely overlooked by the medical field when assessing someone's physical symptoms and experience. Your vagus nerve is getting triggered all the time without you realizing it. When you experience constant triggering of the vagus nerve through trauma and stress it can lead to issues with your throat, stomach, and your vitals. "The vagus nerve is the longest in the ANS. It runs from the brainstem through the neck and abdomen. It carries messages between the brain, digestive system, and organs. It has several vital functions the body relies on daily like gag reflex, slowing your heart rate, regulating your body heat, and controlling your blood pressure levels." (Khiron Clinics, 2022)

Not only that, but this particular nerve is closely related to our mood, and trauma can impact its function. "It plays a role in mental health and well-being as well! Traumatic experiences can contribute to an overactive vagus nerve which leads to anxiety, mood changes, nausea, and pain," (Khiron Clinics, 2022).

Luckily, the act of guided breathing, or breath work, has a big impact on the nerve when it gets agitated. "High levels of stress and anxiety can also trigger the vagus nerve. When it is overstimulated it can cause symptoms like vomiting, dizziness, and abdomen pain. It's possible to soothe and relax the vagus nerve by utilizing breathing exercises that slow the heart rate and relax the body," (Khiron Clinics, 2022). But since not all doctors understand the impact of an irritated Vagus nerve, many people often go to the doctor for these physical symptoms, and are given medication which further upsets the microbiome of the gut creating more issues and continued symptoms. If this is your experience, try deep breathing exercises like those highlighted on my website, which you can access through the **QR** code in the Resources Section. This is not medical advice, but I will say if these are your symptoms and you haven't tried deep breathing exercises, please try them because it might be that simple. Doctors often don't look at the emotional aspect or trauma in someone's experience.

Sometimes, gut and health issues are attributable to nervous system disruptions caused by traumatic experiences. "When the nervous system is overwhelmed by trauma, it can be difficult for people to move back to a state of safety as they are constantly on high alert for danger. Contributing to an overactive vagus nerve causing physical trauma symptoms like unexplained pain and nausea," (Khiron Clinics, 2022). Any level of extended periods of stress and fear will create gut issues and pain in the areas where you hold the emotion or shadow belief that's feeding the pain (fed by you or unconsciously because it has been passed down).

"As the dorsal side of the vagus nerve is on high alert for danger, those who have experienced past trauma can jump immediately into the freeze or immobilization response. They may associate more social cues like a change in tone of voice or body language as dangerous, therefore, freezing to protect themselves from further harm," (Khiron Clinics, 2022). When someone has experienced high levels of trauma for a long time this can also happen, freezing or becoming dissociated in response to certain stimuli. Due to fear and having to read their environment, there will be heightened sensitivity to any changes at all in their environment, which could send a person into dissociation if they hear someone's voice becoming louder or the sound of a door slamming, whether related or not. Their nervous system cannot handle the potential threat and therefore, the program selected in shadow is to shut down, slowing down organ function to go undetected by predators.

Trauma and the Brain

Research and brain scans have shown evidence that the conscious parts of our brain become altered and affected after experiencing trauma. It's important to understand what's happened to your brain if this describes parts of your experience. "Trauma alters the structure and function of the brain. Specifically the neocortex or the rational thinking brain:

amygdala, hippocampus, and prefrontal cortex. All areas are involved in emotional regulation, memory, and decision-making. These changes can lead to symptoms like flashbacks, avoidance behaviors, and difficulty regulating one's emotions," (Understanding Trauma, 2023).

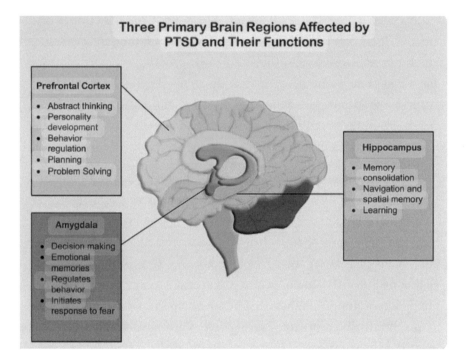

Fig. 8. Nash, Amy. G. "Three Primary Brain Regions Affected by PTSD and Their Functions." 12 Dec 2020, *Amy G Nash Counseling- Licensed Clinical Professional Counselor*, https://www.amygnashcounseling.com/post/what-are-triggers.

"It is difficult to heal from trauma because your nervous system is designed to protect you first and foremost. Think of the brain and nervous system like a computer that runs on electricity, but it also has its own internal programming or backup programs (my term) that control how you function. Trauma can cause this internal or backup programming to go haywire, making healing more difficult than it could be," (Understanding Trauma, 2023).

The brain and nervous system work together constantly to protect us from danger by pushing us into fight or flight mode when faced with an emergency or threat of harm. This response allows us to react quickly when faced with danger, but it also means the body doesn't have time for rational thought processes in times of life-threatening danger in order to save energy for survival (i.e., someone is attacking you). Therefore, your brain utilizes shadow—aka your unconscious and subconscious parts of your brain's previously conditioned programs—to survive, because thinking requires too much energy!

With my clients I'll often use the phrase "flipping their lid" and begin using the hand-brain model[6]. When you're triggered or experience any level of trauma your conscious brain flips offline, leaving only your shadow brain to keep you alive with whatever has been programmed. These are the shadow programs of our subconscious and unconscious brain, and when they activate it feels like autopilot. When this happens, the most ancient parts of your brain are activated combined with your trauma. It uses recorded past programming that's unrelated to what's happening now and you're no longer in the driver's seat. All the while, you think you're actually upset for reasons related to the current situation. In reality, the only thing related is the feeling that came up in response, which is what your shadow projected onto the

---

[6] In the session, I'll even use my hands to show the lid flipping, which is also called "the hand-brain model." One hand is the brainstem and the other is the conscious brain or lid that flips offline when you're triggered.

situation. Oftentimes, you'll end up feeling horrified or embarrassed for how you acted, because it's like you blacked out and were possessed. You probably won't even remember what happened or why you acted that way. I bet you gave yourself hell for those times, too. It's a vicious cycle, and I speak from experience here.

It's trauma and nervous system dysregulation that blocks your access to executive functioning, critical thinking, and conscious awareness. Trauma is what triggers the neocortex or "thinking mind" to go offline. When this happens, the lid is flipped, so to speak, and now you only have what's been previously programmed and exists in shadow outside of your conscious awareness. You can't expect to do anything helpful or new when you're triggered without this one element: *practice*. Think about why crisis intervention specialists like EMS, ER, police and firefighters know how to do their job in traumatic crisis situations. For years, they have to practice these drills, in every scenario, considering every possibility, including distractions, so when the time comes the skills they need are drilled into them.

Reprogramming a person's nervous system and building skills in this way will impact the natural response to traumatic stimuli. Over time, practicing a different set of skills can completely replace the innate survival program through exposure. But you have to practice the skills and information that needs to be accessed frequently and consistently to remain at the forefront of your subconscious shadow mind. If you don't practice consistently, and for an extended period, you'll revert back to your subconscious mind and lose conscious access and retrieval. When you're unaware of the shadow programming and are met with trauma and triggers your body may respond in unhelpful ways.

TRAUMA AND THE BODY

Trauma Body Memory

Trauma gets programmed into your body feeling memory. Body feeling memory is also called somatic memory. This is what happens when held or unrepressed emotional, psychological, or physical trauma remains in the tissues of the body until the opportunity is taken to feel it to release it. For individuals who experience phantom pains or have various pains and physical issues that your doctors can't figure out, or experience dysregulating flashbacks, this section is for you.

"Trauma body memory is used by clinical psychologists and psychiatrists to describe the encoding of past traumatic life events involving fear of death and other serious bodily threats that can cause the most disturbing and persistent impressions on body memory. Traumatic body memories are particularly observed in posttraumatic stress disorder (PTSD) with intrusively re-experienced traumatic life events that manifest in the form of somatic flashbacks including physical sensations such as smells, tastes, pain, haptic experiences, pressure, or sweating. For example, the past experience of pain under torture may reappear in a conflict situation corresponding exactly to the body parts that were affected by the torture," (Jacobsen, 2022).

Trauma and Physical Health Issues

Research has discovered more links between serious health issues and unresolved trauma. "When childhood trauma goes untreated, it can impact physical, mental, and emotional functioning into adulthood. Childhood trauma is linked to an increased risk of numerous physical health problems including cancer, stroke, obesity, diabetes, and heart disease. This is because the chronic stress from trauma elevates levels of stress hormones in the body, which takes its toll over time," (Jacobsen, 2022).

The Conscious Mind

Recent neuroscience and brain scan studies show that we have access to and use only five to ten percent of our conscious awareness at any waking moment. Theoretically, we live 90 to 95 percent in shadow at any waking moment. Dr. Lipton noted "scientific assessment reveals that the wishes, desires, and aspirations of our creative conscious minds only control cognitive behavior about five percent of the time. Subconscious programs are in control of 95% of our lives," (Gustafson, 2017). The parts of the brain that are considered to be conscious are the hippocampus, amygdala, and prefrontal cortex, also called the neocortex or "the lid" (top) of your brain.

Consciousness is related to the thinking, rational mind, critical thinking, problem-solving, deductive reasoning, learning something new, focusing on a task you just learned, short-term memory, and a capacity for alternative interpretations of complex or ambiguous data. For a visual aid, I've borrowed Freud's iceberg concept and updated it, with the top of the iceberg representing the percentage of conscious awareness we have at any waking moment.

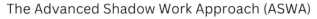

The Advanced Shadow Work Approach (ASWA)

Iceberg Image ©2024 by Courtney Keiser

The Subconscious Mind

Neuroscience and brain scan studies show that we have access to and are utilizing 50-60% of our subconscious mind at any waking moment. It remains largely unknown to our conscious awareness. It influences our thoughts, emotions, and behaviors. It's the autopilot program that comes online when you don't have to think to do something, like breathing. Once we become conscious of it, we can change and control our breathing pattern. It holds all of the backup programs regarding what was modeled for us in behavior, attachment, emotional regulation, and coping mechanisms. Your shadows or trauma live here, along with everything you've ever read, heard, felt, and experienced.

Dr. Lipton says, "of the downloaded behaviors acquired before age seven, the vast majority—70% or more—are programs of limitation, disempowerment, and self-sabotage. These programs were acquired from other people, not from ourselves. Again, being subconscious, these programs are occurring without conscious recognition and awareness. Therefore, though we have a perception in our mind that we are controlling our lives with our wishes and desires, the truth is far from that. Since thought causes 95% of our cognitive behavior to be controlled by the subconscious—i.e. below the conscious mind's "invisible" behaviors, we struggle to manifest our conscious mind's wishes and desires," (Gustafson, 2017).

You can access the subconscious mind at random, when you can never remember the name of that one actor if asked on the spot. Of course, days later, you'll remember his name out of nowhere, long after you needed that nugget of info.

Techniques like Freud's free association (I lovingly refer to it as "word vomit," no offense to psychoanalysis therapists), meaning you express your thoughts and feelings without censoring, can help us access the subconscious. This is where the term "Freudian slip" comes from. Your shadow will say things out loud that you're not yet consciously aware of, which often brings new insight. The downside to this technique is that it doesn't take you into an altered state of consciousness, therefore, the level of accuracy and the amount of access you have will be extremely limited. Because of this, it will likely take you forever to get to the answers you seek.

Unconscious Mind

Neuroscience and brain scan studies show that we have access to and are utilizing 30-40% of our unconscious mind at all times, but some say more. Emma Young states in "New Scientist Magazine" that "current scientific estimates are that some 95% of brain activity is unconscious. These include habits and patterns, automatic body functions, creativity, emotions, personality, beliefs, and values, cognitive biases, and long-term memory. Moreover, up to 40% of behavior is habitual, taking anywhere from 15 to over 250 days to form a new habit," (Young, 2024). If you remember we discussed earlier that your whole body functions because of unconscious systems running at all times. Can you imagine if that wasn't the case and you had to consciously think about chewing and digesting all day? We would literally never get anything done, we'd be digesting 24 hours a day.

There are far more processes and programs stored in the unconscious mind than what our conscious minds can fathom. "Many of the elements that go into judgments and decision-making are processed outside of awareness. Intuition too, is a product of unconscious mental operations, a set of assumptions swiftly assembled from cumulative knowledge and experience. Much of human motivation and interpersonal attraction also take shape beyond conscious awareness," (Unconscious, n.d.).

I theorize that all of our unhealed ancestral, generational, past life, and collective trauma is hidden in shadow programs within our unconscious mind. It's likely most of us would never have found out about our past life and collective trauma on our own. It's only at a certain level in your healing and spiritual practice that you can ask your spirit guides to help you trace the current issue's origin through meditation, channeling, or spiritual plant medicine journeys. You can't consciously be in your unconscious mind. Your conscious mind, the rational mind, has to get out of the way to enter into the unconscious. You will need a professional or specialist who is trained and certified in techniques that aid in entering altered states of consciousness to get the answers you seek like hypnotization, meditation, journeying, and channeling[7].

There are differing opinions in the scientific and psychological communities about whether or not there's a subconscious mind, or if everything outside of consciousness is considered the unconscious mind. At this point, it's all speculation. Both the subconscious and unconscious minds are defined here, but for the purposes of my theory, the two are lumped together as shadow anyway. That's because they're both hidden from conscious awareness and exist in shadow.

Here's a brief example of an unhelpful shadow program that may come online when triggered. Say your boss calls you into their office, you immediately begin to dissociate because you heard a rumor about layoffs. Turns out you were not getting laid off, just touching base, but the surge of fear and jump to a negative conclusion is caused by activated shadow.

A Note From The Author

---

[7] You can enter into altered states of consciousness through intentional practices and forms of meditation or journeying. Working with Goddesses and your spiritual team will allow you to discover what you need to see. It usually takes many years of doing this work to get to this point, but my guides informed me that in the Age of Aquarius, it will not take you as long. That's for another book, but worth mentioning.

Although I'm not a medical doctor, I've observed how many clients' emotional experiences have a direct correlation to various physical health issues they're living with. As they begin to heal emotionally and psychologically, their physical symptoms also heal. Everything is more connected than what we've been led to believe. We must understand this and utilize this information for our highest and greatest good. I'm not saying that I'm a miracle worker. All that I can say for sure is that I've witnessed my clients transform in incredible ways, and I want to impart that wisdom for you to do with as you please.

CHAPTER 5

INTENTION

M ost importantly, you need to be clear on your intention to heal. Why are you doing shadow work? What is the intention, goal, or experience you're hoping to achieve?

First and foremost, you need to heal for yourself and no one else. Don't do it for another person. People will come and go in your life, if you choose to heal for someone else, the healing work you believe you're doing will not become second-order or long-lasting change. The personal investment and value aren't in alignment with longevity or truth if your healing is in service to someone else and not the self.

As soon as that relationship ends, or something happens, most people tend to go back to their old patterns and stop doing shadow work. Since they were never doing it for themselves, they will, of course, abandon themselves. That other person was more important than themselves. The next person, and next person, will be the next more important thing. Clients in these situations tend to continue embracing avoidance until faced with the truth—needing to become their own most important thing. Let me save you some time. Make sure to choose you, you deserve *everything*.

Still, plenty of us begin the healing journey because of issues in our relationships, or because we're unhappy with our behavior or experience in a relationship, career, partnership, friendship, school program, etc. We want to fix things or make them better. We naturally want to help ourselves or help the relationship as a whole. As time goes on, you'll learn and understand your relationships through a much deeper lens during your shadow work. It will eventually become clear to you that you don't need fixing; you will realize that the healing begins and ends with you.

When we focus on ourselves and our own healing then we can truly look at our own behavior instead of what the other person is doing. All we can control is our own behavior. When we create a clear intention around why we're doing this work, it uncovers a lot of information about the shadow programs you could be working with and the ones that may pop up during your work.

This is the process of asking yourself introspective questions and learning more about your behavior, as well as your attachments, patterns, emotions, and the triggers you're experiencing. It means clearly identifying the problem areas you have in your life—areas of struggle, stagnation, frustration, feeling like not enough or unworthy, fear, pain, anger, and any feelings of being blocked.

It's okay if you don't have a super specific goal, it could be to become more consciously aware and be more trusting of yourself. Maybe you just want to love yourself or see if that's even possible. Over time, the answer and intention will become very clear and take you down various routes of healing towards that desired goal. You may even start with one goal and realize it's another. Either way, the truth will be revealed. Try to remain open to what truth is being illuminated.

Lastly, set intentions that are positive and that honor your highest good and the highest good of all with integrity and love. You're amazing, let's make incredible things happen for you!

CHAPTER 6

GROUNDING & COPING SKILLS

I honestly cannot say enough how important it is to have solid grounding and coping skills, not only to exist in this crazy, triggering, beautiful, magikal world, but to make a difference in your life and your shadow work, it is *essential*.

I have a golden rule that I fully believe in and stick to when it comes to shadow work. If you don't have any grounding skills, or don't already practice grounding and coping skills, I suggest working with a mental health professional or making it your top priority to learn and practice some skills daily. It will make a night and day difference in your shadow work journey, *trust me*. I don't like wasting time, especially my own. I'm not going to waste yours.

You must have the skills to ground before you begin doing shadow work. And please, for the love of Goddess, don't use a shadow work workbook if you don't know how to self-soothe in a healthy and effective way. I'm not judging you or shaming you. I'm here to protect you and tell you the truth, because others have chosen not to. If you don't know how to help yourself and the workbook doesn't provide you with these life-saving skills, doing that will re-traumatize you and cause setbacks. Practice these skills, they will save your life many times over.

As I mentioned earlier, I always ask clients in their first session what coping and grounding skills they use. How often do they use them? What situations or emotions do they work best for? What other ones do they use? What grounding and coping skills work best with these specific emotions or triggers? What do they usually do when they are triggered? How do they support themselves? Do they actually try to help themselves calm down or what is the pattern of how they show up for their emotions and nervous system regulation needs? Do they feel they might abandon, deny, reject, and avoid them? What would your answers be to these questions? Can you have compassion and acceptance for yourself while you answer them truthfully?

What I've discovered is that most people claim to practice coping and grounding skills, but they don't. They typically regurgitate mainstream techniques they learned online, from their therapist, or read in a book. They rarely characterize legitimate coping and grounding skills that effectively work for all emotions and intensities.

I'm not suggesting that all therapists don't provide sound grounding skills to their clients. Quite the contrary, it's that the clients tend to not actually use them. Therefore, they don't remember what their therapist suggested, so they list exercises they have heard about or have been programmed in their subconscious mind and shadow that are helpful, like walking, listening to music, being in nature, going for a drive, or deep breathing. These are all helpful things, unless you're in extreme rage, despair, panic, or fear. Those listed skills are laughable when it comes to coping with emotions of those intensities. This tells me that the client doesn't know how to support all of their emotions and needs help building a window of tolerance through grounding skills, coping skills, and self-talk.

Furthermore, the dissemination of incorrect information surrounding grounding practices can unintentionally fuel further avoidance and escapism tactics that don't meet the required emotional and somatic needs to heal. The programmed shadow response, that we've unknowingly been conditioned to believe and function in, is one that rejects, avoids, and fears our emotional experiences while denying that we need any help regulating ourselves. Most people are so stuck in their stress response that they don't even realize they're at an eleven when they think they are at a grounded two. I find people are often very disconnected from their own bodies and nervous systems. I say this not to shame or judge, but to normalize that this is just about everyone's experience at some point and all levels are welcome.

Anyone can say 'yes I practice these things,' because we all have a level of shadow programmed bias to lie and manipulate, to control others' perceptions of how we want to be seen. People want me to think they practice these skills, which helps no one. I'll keep asking in different ways. The more specific I get, I start to see panic in their face as they wrestle with how to tell me they don't help themselves self-soothe when they need it.

The truth that often comes out is, "I know what I could do, but I actually don't do anything to help myself. I just kind of ignore it and binge-watch shows, distract myself, exercise, or go out drinking with my friends." I reply with, "I already know, I'm not judging you. It's hard to break patterns and help ourselves in a society that never taught us how." That's when I explain collective shadow programs and alleviate some pressure, because it's not our fault this has been conditioned and programmed into all of us.

But we can choose to take accountability, build our awareness, and take responsibility to do something about it. You can pour love into yourself as you come to understand that this is your ancestor's pain. They suffered because of horrendous oppression and abuse from the church and the patriarchy's violent rules that involved hunting women, killing those who had deeply felt expressive realities full of power, and blinding our unique gifts and connection to all. They lacked support, and in turn, learned to deny their feelings to survive and stay alive. That leads to an inherent belief you'll naturally express, generations later, of living small, trapped in shame and fear.

It's time to love yourself so much more than your ancestors ever knew that they could. Give yourself the voice and freedom to express and feel your truth. Your ancestors will feel all of that love and freedom, I promise you. I know this to be true because they tell me and show me each time we break the chains of the past.

There is power in visualization meditation, where you can visualize your shadow self connected to your ancestors. As you show your shadow that deep love and acceptance, your ancestors are also receiving that love and acceptance. I watch them light up with warmth and love at seeing you and watch their chains disappear.

Fig. 18. "Chart: How Meditation Unleashes Subconscious Mind Power." 13 April 2024, *EOC Institute,*
https://eocinstitute.org/meditation/how-to-harness-your-subconscious-mind-power/.

As humans, we cycle through emotions, quickly moving past feelings we'd rather avoid or ignore. Grounding and coping skills make it so you can actually feel your emotions and release them. This is a tactic that leads to real change, instead of extending the inevitable over and over again. It helps you develop a window of tolerance.

This is where my sense of urgency (besides Spirit nudging me) in writing this book comes from, particularly after I saw a new shadow workbook came out. I've only seen one workbook that I can recommend, because she actually provides QR codes for grounding and coping skills exercises, "The Shadow Work Journal: A Guide to Integrate and Transcend Your Shadows" by Keila Shaheen. That's the only way to do it if you're going to make it a workbook. There could be more of them out there that are helpful, and I know each of the authors means well. For the millions of eyes it has brought to this work, I'm grateful. But let's do it the appropriate way—we're dealing with people's trauma. Part of working from the mindset of the highest good of all is knowing the consequences that can arise from not being fully aware of the responsibility inherent in dealing with an individual's trauma.

I don't believe we have to revisit the trauma itself or the incident(s) in particular to heal and alchemize the trauma. With that said, I truly believe that no shadow work should ever be practiced solely on your own. As in, you don't meet with a professional one time during your life. A professional can help you tap into altered states of consciousness that you will 100% need, they can help you access the answers you seek that you will never be able to reach on your own. Sometimes, it's useful to have a practitioner help you discover new shadows along the way, or offer support if you need help with self-talk, etc.

The most important reason why we practice grounding and coping skills is to prevent you from being constantly re-traumatized. It will build trust with your shadows and with yourself. By keeping yourself safe and grounded, you're truly taking care of yourself and your needs. You got your own back. To build solid foundations and relationships with your shadows, they need to trust that you're there for them and that when they're triggered or upset, you'll help them ground. You'll feel incredible about it because they're so grateful that you care and haven't forgotten about them. It's because change, and even just looking at ourselves honestly, is extremely hard for most.

To break patterns and cycles, and not revert to unhealthy toxic behaviors and shadow programs is incredibly hard. To revert is the easiest choice, it takes less effort, but it also creates heftier consequences. Navigating big life transitions as you evolve into newer, truer versions of yourself will be possible only if you have these skills. It will allow you to transform your life so it resonates with your current and future self. With grounding and coping skills, we can surrender to the cycles of life instead of resisting them.

Just as things that need to come to an end do, when we're grounded, we can approach change with greater grace. We can begin to realize that the less we resist, the faster the change happens, which allows a higher vibration and vibrancy to enter into your life. This is why grounding is my golden rule. Even if you decide shadow work isn't for you, or that therapy, or healing yourself isn't for you, that's fine. All I care about is that you know how to ground and cope. These skills are beneficial to everyone no matter their circumstance. This is one way we break ancestral, generational, collective, and past life trauma. These are life skills that everyone can use to navigate the ups and downs of life, the challenges, surprises, endings, transitions, and changes. Imagine if everyone practiced grounding in their lives. How much lovelier would the world be?

Another good reminder before going into shadow work is to remember to be mindful of your own energy and to not push yourself to be constantly doing the deep exploratory work. In the beginning, people are eager to learn, grow, and transform. I get it—when you begin to taste the spiritual energy, feel your conscious power, and your awareness grows, you feel a new zest for life. The progress pumps you up with each "aha" moment. I guarantee that you will become a student of life yet again, one that wants to dive deeper. There's a reason why we only have access to five to ten percent of our conscious awareness at one time. People don't realize how exhausting and draining this work is. Not because of the crying and trauma, but because it takes massive amounts of energy and vitality to be in your conscious mind more. It's exhausting to try to actively think and function from a place of intention and emotional intelligence. We function at five to ten percent because it's optimal for our energetic balance in the human body to not overload the nervous system.

I theorize that as souls we are pure consciousness. That it's not the objective of living this life as a human to become fully conscious. You also don't want to. There are many wonderful things happening on a shadow or unconscious level, like digestion, that you don't need to be aware of. You would become aware of too many things that would take so much of your energy and focus away from the mission of attuning to yourself versus something menial like digestion.

We're meant to become more conscious and connected with self, Source, and Mother Nature. It's the human ego or shadow that wants access to full consciousness without knowing what that really means. We aren't meant to have all the answers. Ego always wants the most; to be the most informed or "woke." We heal and as a result, we become more conscious. Then, it becomes the goal to become even *more* conscious, until you realize that it just means becoming more in tune with all that is, but in a more conscious way. Always expanding and evolving. Yes, we want to become more aware of our behavior, our impact, our choices, and the consequences of karma for self and others. We need to learn there's also magik and balance in surrendering to what is, and not trying to control an outcome or goal. The real goal is to be consciously flowing with life and making intentional actions as you co-create your magikal life with the universe. But stress and anxiety about achieving this will have a direct effect on your gut biome and how it functions. We don't want to start having digestion and tummy problems as a result of shadow work.

Relating this back to grounding, it's okay to slow down and take your time with this. There's no reason to give yourself anxiety to get through it quickly, because you'll also miss a lot of lessons if you go too fast. That sense of urgency is stress culture, so work to sit through the uncomfortability with deep belly breathing, shaking, sacred rage release, NLP (non-linguistic programming), EFT or tapping, or any other exercise you feel called to ground with.

Our human minds say the most. When we drop the attachment to the outcome, or having any semblance of control over it, especially if it feeds the ego, and instead choose to ground in order to help ourselves, we can surrender to what is. Wanting to succeed in shadow work means knowing there is no goal. That's why there is no destination. It doesn't work like that. It's not a physical thing we can measure and quantify, or even wrap our heads around what it even means.

As you dig into your work, you'll find yourself exhausted, likely for a few weeks or even a few months, depending on how deeply you go in before realizing that you overwhelmed your nervous system. This intense feeling comes with a greater awareness, as we're opening up our senses to take in and process more information—behaviors of self and others, intention, energy, sounds, smells, feelings, sense of knowing, and just about everything is heightened.

You're feeling drained because you've been using more energy to be in your conscious brain while building your level of awareness. You can get confused at times, or not see the full picture, because you're trying to speed through the process to get to a goal. You need to allow yourself intentional breaks, otherwise you're going to be in a constant state of depletion. Break away from constant mind mapping, from exploring deeper meanings and seeking answers within.

Of course, I encourage you to be as aware as you can be, but in the beginning you don't want to overdo it just because you see progress or find answers. It's okay, you're excited, it happens to everyone. But you have to allow space for rest, and meditation to support new brain cell and neural pathway growth, which is exactly why I emphasize that so much. Grounding will amplify any higher goals, guidance, and growth you're seeking.

Meditation can extend consciousness, allowing you to connect to higher wisdom and receive guidance. It also allows you to let go and relax. It can support either mode. Listen to what your body and nervous system are telling you, it will be a process of learning what that means.

For the purposes of this book, I won't go into detail about all of the specific coping and grounding skills, but instead list just a few of my favorites. For those of you who are interested in learning more about specific grounding skills, you can access those via the **QR** code in the resources section. I don't have every grounding and coping skill listed and it's not a one-size-fits-all process either. If you didn't find something that honors your needs, advocate for yourself and keep searching on the internet, find a professional, or keep seeking until you find something that works for you. Something exists, I promise you.

The most commonly known examples of grounding and coping skills are types of breathwork, meditation, and somatic practices. Often, people think there's only one kind of meditation, when there's actually a spectrum to choose from and explore. I have eight different types of meditation listed in my class and on my website. If you've ever been frustrated trying to meditate, was it because you couldn't stand to sit in silence, and were perhaps flooded by a stream of constantly revolving thoughts? Well, I have good news for you. You were attempting the hardest kind of meditation, which is really only attainable for advanced, skilled meditators.

Practice Movement Meditation: Instead, I would encourage you to try a different form of meditation that better resonates with you. Frequently, I refer beginners towards movement meditation as an intuitive way to reconnect with your body. Movement meditation is an active form of meditation where the movement guides you into a deeper connection with your body, the Earth, and the present moment. This includes things like intentionally and mindfully walking, gardening, tai chi, qi gong, or other gentle forms of movement. It's a helpful practice for people who find peace in action and who want to develop body awareness. *For specific meditation exercises and audio guides you can scan the QR code in the resources section for access.*

Practice Abdominal Breathing: In terms of breathwork, I always say that abdominal breathing, or deep belly breathing, is key. This type of breathing activates your vagus nerve telling your nervous system that you're safe. It works very quickly to regulate the body and bring the emotions back down to a more manageable place, where you can think or move through the situation. Place one hand on your heart and the other on your belly and breathe as normal. Notice which hand raises more than the other. If the hand on your heart is rising higher, focus your inhale on filling the belly with air, pushing the belly out visibly. Then exhaling, pushing all of the air out. Repeat this for five to ten minutes until calm.

The grounding and coping skills that changed my relationship to trauma work in my own healing—but also for many of my clients—were somatic exercises. These exercises help move stuck energy and emotions out of the body, all the while bringing you back into connection with your body.

Somatic exercises are what helped me finally transmute my emotions. It's exactly what I needed to get out of my intellectual brain and back into my feeling body. I'm so grateful for somatic therapies and practices. The somatic practice that I most often suggest to clients is sacred rage release. I've mentioned it throughout this book and firmly believe in its power to transform. There are many ways to do sacred rage release, but this is the most simple way anyone can do it.

The practice and act of sacred rage release brings up a lot of shadows for people. Even if you're alone, it feels as if people are watching you. Feelings of embarrassment creep in, self judgment, fear of looking insane or crazy, and a fear of one's rage. It's fascinating to witness the hundreds of men and women that I've seen this happen to each time. It feels like a sea of people watching us when we're alone, it's bizarre. Push past it.

The level of shame and embarrassment we feel for using our voice, activating our voice, and being wild and free with our voice makes this practice initially feel deeply wrong. That's the shadow program of centuries of oppression and abuse by the patriarchy to keep us in line, submissive, without a voice, powerless, and fearing our own rage so we don't rise against them. These are all things to be aware of and notice what stories come up for you.

You may not hear the stories, but you will feel the feelings. Can you guess what stories and narratives from your ancestors or past lives might be connected to those feelings? Can you show yourself more grace and support to push through the discomfort and encourage the bravery to go there and scream? You won't be the same after and you will wonder what took you so long to try it.

Practice Sacred Rage Release Indoors: First and foremost, if you live in an apartment or townhouse where you share a wall with neighbors, it's smart to let them know that you're doing a therapeutic exercise involving scream release to help regulate your emotional experience. Let them know that you don't want to scare them, that you're okay and no one is getting harmed or needs help. If you don't do this, your neighbors will run from you and never talk to you again (like mine did) or even call the cops. If you live with other people, tell them the same thing. If you live with pets, place them out of the room so everyone is safe and no one gets hurt or upset. Make sure your space is safe, and that you aren't going to trip, fall, or hit something you don't want to hit like breakable objects.

To intentionally release this rage or pent-up anger, you want to focus on what those feelings are and what situations bring them up to the surface. It's a good idea to listen to music that pumps you up and puts you in a mood to release. Maybe do some rounds of breath of fire to activate that fire energy of rage within. When you release, you can be screaming in general or screaming words at that person you wanted to yell at while hitting your pillow as hard as you can. Swing it at your bed. As you scream and are using the energy to hit your bed, send that energy out of you and down into the earth's molten core to be released and transmuted into pure potential. If you don't feel safe to scream without the pillow, scream into the pillow then hit your pillow on the bed in between screams. You should be very sweaty, out of breath, more than likely crying, vibrating, tired, and feel very different afterward. Then journal about your experience.

Practice Sacred Rage Release Outdoors: If you want to take your sacred rage release outside, you definitely could if you're somewhere in the wilderness with privacy where the cops aren't going to get called on you. Collect five to eight sticks that feel good to you to hit against the earth as you scream. These should be the length of baseball bats, but not very thick so they can break. Doing this exercise outside in nature feels even more carnal, wild, and freeing. The medicine that Mother Nature can provide to you as she supports you in your deep release is unparalleled.

Practice Earthing and Ground with Earth Energy: One of my favorite grounding and coping skills that's free and provides numerous benefits in one experience is grounding with earth energy. One method is earthing, which is walking or standing barefoot out in nature to connect with the electrically conductive magnetic field with electrons that pass through the bottoms of your feet promoting intriguing physiological changes and well-being.

Evidence suggests that the Earth's negative potential can create a stable internal bioelectrical environment for the normal functioning of all body systems. Earthing or grounding: Walking barefoot outside connects you to conductive systems that transfer the Earth's electrons from the ground into the body. The benefits are: Better sleep, reduced pain, and oscillations of the intensity of the Earth's potential may be important for setting biological clocks to regulate diurnal body rhythms like cortisol secretion (stress). The influx of free electrons absorbed into the body through direct contact with the Earth neutralizes free radicals, which can reduce acute and chronic inflammation. It also leads to shifts from sympathetic to parasympathetic tone in the autonomic nervous system and causes a blood thinning effect. Blood thinning helps in the prevention of heart attacks, strokes, and blockages by helping keep blood clots from forming.

I hope you find that grounding and coping skills are what's been missing in your daily life. You create a beautiful, trusting bond with yourself and your shadows if you show up for yourself by providing the support you need to do this work. These skills are a gift that society didn't give us, but they're the gift you can now give to yourself. Meet yourself with patience and compassion as you navigate the journey of utilizing grounding and coping skills.

It's always going to be a process to figure out what works best for you. Try as many of these different skills as you can for each of your triggers and emotions. Utilize the forms provided through QR codes for the progress sheets to track what you uncover. To be your best self-healer, you'll want to become an expert to fast track and simplify things for yourself as you figure out your system.

Think about what it would be like to say, "When I'm furious, rage release helps me the most. When I'm sad and feeling hard on myself EFT helps the most. When I'm anxious or stressed belly breathing and a movement meditation combination helps the most. When I'm feeling overwhelmed and stressed I ground in nature and belly breathe while utilizing visualization meditation to send roots down into the earth to ground. Journaling helps me achieve clarity and feel grounded." I bet you would feel so supported. It's possible for you too, because if you know what helps you the most, it means you do it to help yourself. Which leads me to my next tip—timing. Timing is everything.

If you always wait until you're already triggered, furious, or upset to try and use these skills when you haven't been actively using them, you'll forget how to use them or that they even exist. You must practice them regularly and frequently. How will you know it's time to actually use them? Complete the daily check-in form listed in the QR section. The daily check-ins will help you see how there are many signals we're missing that show us we're already dysregulated and need our grounding skills *before* the triggering event happens and sends us into a meltdown.

The goal is to address your nervous system needs as they arise now, rather than only when they're on overload. If you're maintaining your nervous system regulation through a consistent grounding practice, then you're going to be grounded more frequently in general, and it actually becomes more difficult to get to an eleven state of dysregulation at all. The mindset that we should wait until crisis mode to get help is Western society's collective shadow program. This broken model is set up to utterly ignore our nervous system and emotions until they scream at us. It's actually just like the way we've been shadow programmed to approach our overall health and our bodies. So, here we are bringing in the new program, a prevention model that addresses the root problem, instead of avoidance, denial, and rejection.

No healing or growth can happen if the nervous system doesn't feel safe. First, we have to address the nervous system's needs before diving into trauma healing. Please practice these skills as much as you can. Your ability to navigate life's transitions, growth, healing, and challenges all depend on how well you can ground and cope. You need to be able to sit with the process long enough to receive the wisdom of the experiences and the medicine it will bring into your life. It will also be the thing that exponentially grows the trust between yourself and your shadows.

CHAPTER 7

THE POWER OF AWARENESS
& SELF-TALK

W ithout awareness and positive, compassionate, loving, empathetic self-talk you will not master shadow work.

This is where it's necessary to have a professional come in and help you see the things you don't have access to. To be completely transparent with you, you already know the answer you're looking for. We often choose not to trust, or believe there's no way this thing could be the answer, because we don't want it to be, or because of the attachment and meaning we've created around that thing. Sometimes we reject the truth because we have a biased opinion based in shadow. It's okay, we all do it.

We've learned from society, the media, and collective conditioning what it looks like to be a functioning, successful, "good person," and how to fulfill that role within our personal and professional lives. Rather than accepting everyone as unique, there's more of a drive towards a homogenized culture. This toxic mentality is about conformity, powerlessness, consumerism, capitalism, greed, materialism, raping the Earth of her resources, gentrification, and sexism. It's also patriarchal.

We expose our subconscious minds on a daily basis to social media scrolling, news, music, digital content, binge-watching, and podcasts—constantly taking in passive information that impacts our self-talk and awareness on many levels. It becomes evident that we're intentionally distracted by consumerism, addictions, vanity, etc. to keep us imprinted, unaware, and programmable, i.e. far from knowing and healing our true selves.

For example, a person who struggles with low self-confidence, engaging with the sensory overload that's inherent in ordinary life could cause them to cling to the idea of perfection even more. Many people believe something is inherently wrong with them for not being the same as what they see on social media or in mainstream culture.

Women have long been targeted for their ancient wisdom and the magikal power they hold. Most women don't know that we're sacred wisdom keepers with magnanimous healing powers. We're one with the divine mother of the land we walk upon. Women have the power to create life and bring physical beings into this world. When that portal is not being used for a baby, it can birth into the world any project or creation they're passionate about through intentional manifestation practice and focused energetic alignment through actions, thoughts, beliefs, and behaviors.

Before this current patriarchal age, we were once a matriarchal society, one that has almost no traces of written evidence due to the Christian cleansing, which eradicated much of all previous religious ideologies and accompanying texts.

The blasphemous, insufferable oppression of women continues to this day. Women have been oppressed for far too long, which is why we think we're so far removed from our power. That's what they would like us to believe anyway. We're not really separate at all.

We've been conditioned by the people in power, who control the media, to believe that we're sick, fat, old, and going to die any second. The messages we constantly receive are that a crisis could happen to you, or next door, at any moment. These constant fear-based messages create stress, depression, overwhelm, disconnection from self, anxiety, scarcity, and a belief that we're broken. These lies are what fill our thoughts and become the self-talk that's playing on a loop in the background. That loop informs our daily lives, and we may only even be aware of a tiny sliver of it. That's why we spend so much time and emphasis on self-talk.

That's why self-talk will determine exactly how your shadow work journey will be experienced.

Collectively, as a society, there are many ways that shadow programs show up in our individual lives through self-talk.

As mentioned, the collective trauma of oppression has transformed into self-oppression and betrayal. There's plenty of self-oppression that expresses low self-worth: "I'm not worthy, I'm never going to get that job, they will never pick me, he will never choose me, I never get anything, there's nothing I can do about it, I don't have any power in this, no one will believe me anyway, no one cares, why even try? It doesn't make a difference what I do, I never get what I want. I'm ugly, fat, stupid, a failure. I'm worthless. I'm supposed to suffer. Nothing good comes easy."

A form of collective religious trauma also lives in us all, no matter what religion you practice or don't practice, unless you're a brand new soul, you have this trauma in you. This is expressed through shame, guilt, living small and being small, being modest and preferring to go unnoticed because that's "humble and not shameful." This is also expressed through the idea that caring for yourself is selfish, and that differences in choices and people you don't understand means you should respond in fear by projecting shame, hate, judgment, and guilt. This looks like a lot of self-shaming language. "I can't wear that, that's not ladylike. I can't say that and talk out of turn. The man is the leader of the home. The woman or wife has a role to fulfill." There's still a lot of shame surrounding how women dress and how they exhibit themselves in public and in relationships.

The shadow program of being a "good girl" or a "good person" means you slut and sex shame yourself. This self-talk comes up a lot around body image, how you look or dress, your sexuality, or your gender. Leaning towards being more wild and true to yourself by embracing your spirituality might bring up these shadows. Thoughts like, "I'm going to go to hell for being gay. I'm a terrible person, I'm such a whore what is wrong with me? I would rather be the unhappiest person in the world than get a divorce and find happiness because I was married under the 'eyes of God.'" You may have internal anger or rage about religion for no apparent reason (you think) and want to support the opposite side of the spectrum, but that's still a response from the shadow, because it speaks from past life wounding that you're not yet free from.

It also looks like collective bias as a shadow program—we're taught to deny our shadow's existence. We adopt socially acceptable lies to tell the people we're connecting with. We're taught to lie to ourselves, to judge ourselves for being different or not doing things how we're told to do them, and to deny ourselves our true experiences. Through this denial, most people don't return to it and say "Okay, I noticed bias—let me look into that." They will continue to skim right over it and pretend it doesn't exist. We've all been conditioned to say this to each other for some reason, "Hi, how are you?" "I'm good, how are you?" "I'm good, thank you!" *Why?* I wonder how many times both people are not doing good, but smile and say they are. This bias says only show your best self, only your best is accepted. Don't let anyone see you when you're not being perfect, messing up, or having a learning moment (mistake). This programming can sound like the following: "Don't be like that, be good, not bad, be submissive and easily conditioned to follow orders, and don't cause trouble," etc.

When trying to answer questions honestly, many people's initial reaction is to say the truth, but then they refrain because they judge their truth. They would rather manipulate the answer to appear more favorable in someone else's eyes because they're judging themselves and believing that many things about them are unacceptable or wrong. This only creates more self-shame and lower self-worth. Goddess forbid someone finds out you don't meditate every day.

Politeness and etiquette, southern charm, and surface driven "water cooler" or weather talk are examples of where the collective has been conditioned and programmed to lie to others right off the bat. We don't even genuinely invest in creating real conversations. We all loathe the facade, but yet we all still engage in this behavior. Why do we do this?

It happens through shadow, subconsciously, and it's been repeated so many times now that it's second nature. But you can become aware of it just by being mindful of your thoughts when you engage in conversation. It's okay that it happens, but the goal is to try to get to a place where we can all relate and communicate more genuinely and authentically, so you can also learn that you're not supposed to be like others. Be different, be unique, and stop judging yourself, please.

This is usually where I like to have some fun in conversation, to really resist conformity so that I can create more meaningful connections. It can be awkward. You have to be mindful if you have a shadow to overshare or try to manipulate others to feel bad for you, etc. Therefore, it's important to be aware of how you communicate where you are and how you would handle a few different possible responses. I'm just straight up honest when someone asks, "How are you?" I'll say this if it's true, "I'm not having the best day, but I'm getting through. Thank you for asking." or "I'm having a rough day, but I'm here and I'm grateful to be alive."

At first, it was ancestral trauma, then it was passed down as generational trauma, now, it's expressed on the collective scale as denial and avoidance of emotions through repression, suppression, and escapism—literal fleeing, ghosting, avoiding, addictions, toxic coping strategies (drugs, alcohol, sex).

Many people not only ignore the feelings they're having, they proclaim to not have any emotions or feelings. Pretending like things aren't bothering them while they invariably are. These festering emotions fuel negative self-talk. Many of us gaslight and dismiss our feelings, psychologically abusing ourselves daily.

A lot of people don't realize the toll it takes on the whole system to ignore your feelings. This only further leads you to believe "I'm not safe with myself. I'm not safe to feel my emotions because I don't accept them. Why waste my time? I don't do anything about it or help myself, I just need to stay busy and keep my mind off of it." You hide from your unacknowledged emotions with more distractions, more tasks, and more projects to do. We live in the era of productivity to avoid feeling.

The avoidance of feeling emotions and moving through them was the golden rule for our parent's generation. It's not their fault that they weren't taught how to feel and acknowledge their emotions without fear of abuse or neglect from their parents or caregivers.

The further back in time you go through the generations, the greater and more horrific the abuse and neglect were in the home and the external environment (not for all families but as a collective this is a common story). Life was about doing what you had to do to survive. That's the thinking that was programmed into our parents and ultimately us.

When this stuff comes up and you want to avoid it, remember to have some grace with yourself. You have your back up against centuries of toxic programming and trauma. All of this didn't come from your life. You're not the problem. You are the *solution*. Be kinder, more supportive, encouraging, positive, and patient in your self-talk. When you become more aware, the safer you will feel to acknowledge your emotions, because you'll feel seen and heard, not judged, denied, and abandoned.

Various forms of media are constantly being programmed into your subconscious mind. These messages influence your beliefs, desires, wants, needs, connection or disconnection with self and others, behaviors, habits, communication, self-talk, perspective, openness, acceptance, tolerance, ability to emotionally regulate or to know you need that. That's why it's imperative to become a conscious participant in choosing what you're passively programming yourself with, from what you watch, to the music you listen to, it all matters and affects your energetic vibration.

We can choose to become more accountable and responsible for our behavior and way of living, even if we never experienced loving and nurturing communication before. Please don't let that stop you.

I've helped so many people who have never experienced loving self-talk learn how to provide it for themselves. It's a beautiful thing and I relish the challenge. Most of us weren't lucky enough to grow up with emotionally intelligent parents who know how to self-regulate, or help anyone regulate for that matter.

I will lovingly remind everyone, once again, that we only have access to five to ten percent of conscious awareness at all times. That's not a lot, but because of a wonderful thing we call neuroplasticity in the brain, it allows for new neural pathways to form. This means new behaviors, patterns, thoughts—everything. These new models replace the old pathways, but only with consistent repetition will they stay in the forefront of your subconscious mind to be easily accessed. The saying, "you can't teach an old dog new tricks" is incorrect. You can learn new behaviors and programs at any age, human or dog. This same rule applies to coping and grounding skills.

There's a collective shadow pattern of attachment. It's related to generations of repression surrounding the fear of letting go, grief and loss, and not feeling and releasing pain and negative emotions. It stems from not moving through the trauma in a healthy way, but instead holding it in, with a fear that letting it go would erase the memory. Over time, this creates a shadow pattern of behavior that looks like a stubborn attachment to certain habits. We emotionally attach these behaviors to our identity or our sense of self. Therefore, if we're stripped of them we experience panic, anxiety, and fear.

An example of how the shadow pattern of attachment could be expressed is through unhealthy coping mechanisms that are passed down like hoarding and collecting items, severe anxiety and depression—which can be triggered and exacerbated by deep intense feelings related to attachment to people, places, things— and how we react when faced with grief and loss.

Once you have successfully learned what's in your highest good and the highest good of all, and chosen yourself, that test will no longer be presented to you. You will graduate from that lesson. You'll start to align with and become more aware of the higher vibrational things all around you that you were previously unaware of.

It's pretty wild when you become aware of the dance of energetic alignment to receive what you desire. If you're not in resonance with those higher vibrational waves in terms of your actions, behavior, thoughts, emotions, and beliefs, the Universe will cloak what you want, making it invisible until you align with it. When you're in alignment, it appears, and seemingly falls into your lap. It's like a slap in the face every time like "that's right it's that easy!" We've been conditioned to believe that everything is meant to be difficult.

Self-talk can change the entire course and trajectory of your life. It's so interesting to see the difference between people who are aware of this versus people who aren't. It fascinates me. When you choose to be brave and acknowledge that you need empathetic, nurturing self-talk that's also real, honest, non-judgemental, accepting, and wise, you'll feel confused as to why you didn't try this sooner. You'll wonder why you fought so hard to deny doing this for yourself.

In every phase of your life, you'll be making minor adjustments to your self-talk based on who you have become, what your shadows need now, words that resonate with you now, concepts or ideas that you're connecting to as you continue to expand and grow your consciousness and understanding of yourself, life, the universe, and your purpose.

Speaking out loud makes a difference. There's something about audibly hearing it that registers somewhere different in your brain, telling you it's coming from outside of you. It's like your brain thinks that it's someone else saying it, because your voice tends to come from within and stay silent to everyone else.

If you don't care about what people think and you unapologetically show up for yourself and your needs no matter what, you might be the most incredible person on Earth. It's so metal to radically fulfill your own needs. That's what used to be natural, until it was programmed out of us throughout our patriarchal history. Now is your time to reclaim what you've forgotten, and honor your ancient inner wisdom.

That's what I want to advise all of you to do, move toward a life where you don't give much credence to what others think. If you're doing something that helps you and your highest good, that's the most attractive quality. Showing up for your own emotional needs when it's inconvenient, not ideal, and challenging, is difficult. Wherever you are, you can also always excuse yourself and take a moment in private as well.

You know each other well, since you're the same person, but your shadows don't know you or trust you, so you can't just jump in and randomly try to engage with your shadows without any emotion behind it. If you just read the words someone else wrote off of your phone or a page, it doesn't do anything. It doesn't mean anything to you.

You will probably need to play around with how to be real with yourself without bullying, criticizing, judging, abusing, abandoning, and gaslighting your shadow in the process. If you don't realize you're doing any of the above, then you're likely unaware that shadow is happening and you're not aware of your self-talk. That's okay! You will be aware of it now because I mentioned it.

You have to start somewhere. Be compassionate and patient. This is why it takes people a hot minute to figure out positive self-talk. Once they do, they get in a groove, and their shadow work and healing take off.

Long story short, you probably know when you're being fed bullshit and someone is straight-up lying to your face. Especially if that person is, you know, yourself. You will know. So be real, call yourself out, be gentle, toot your horn, validate those feelings, and let them guide how you're going to move through this emotion. This is a blueprint for what you need to keep doing as you move forward.

Trust me, so much is working against you. This is not a one-and-done practice. It's a lifelong journey. It's an eternal commitment to loving and helping yourself. It's almost like when you decide to be a parent. You can't just decide you're not one anymore when things get hard.

If your parent(s) did abandon you, I'm sorry that was your reality. But if so, you know what that feels like, so don't repeat the pattern by doing the thing that traumatized you in the first place. We tend to do that with our patterns. If we want to break them we have to do the work. This is the work. This is the first time most people learn what it means to be the parent you always needed, and still need, and a strategy around how to do it without the shadow of self-sabotage.

When you're reliable and consistent, that builds security, safety, trust, mutual respect, comfortability, love, and genuine care for each other's well-being. Once your shadows trust you, shadow work starts getting a hell of a lot easier and smoother. That's why self-talk is the biggest challenge because people get in their own way and block their own vision of the answer they already know.

Once your shadow stops coming out and reacting, you may feel like it has healed or left the building. Think again. Just because you're feeling better doesn't mean that you got what you wanted from your shadow and now you can abandon it. Just like anywhere else in this work, when we're building new patterns of behavior and ways of being, it takes consistent practice. Build trust so you can rely on yourself to show up when you need it.

The Universe will test you—your shadow will rear its ugly head to force you to adjust and reassess how you're showing up for yourself. It will ask you to fully commit to the work and yourself. It's a journey of learning how to be grateful for those times, and to help you remember and become aware without falling into old patterns that encourage you to take it out on yourself or others.

When you get to a good, consistent and reliable place with your self-talk, and when you're seeing and feeling the progress, that usually means your energy has adjusted to the intensity required to be more conscious. You're learning to utilize positive self-talk and its power in manifestation and dreaming your life into reality, effectively aligning your self-talk with your desired future to call it in.

It's difficult to have an unwavering belief in yourself through all of the hard times of struggle without losing faith in your dream. It has to come true. You have no other choice than to believe in your dream, because you've committed your whole life to it for however long.

We entered into the Age of Aquarius on November 19, 2024. Get ready for a wild energetic ride for the next 20 years. Be in alignment with your truth, be a rebel, and don't follow the herd. Listen to your intuition and higher self. Help yourself ground and quiet your mind to connect with your higher wisdom.

The Age of Aquarius brings us into a period when we will manifest at lightning speed. Therefore, it's pertinent that we all become more aware of where our energy and mind go, so that we can be present in the reality that we're constantly co-creating with the Universe.

Below is The Age of Aquarius Seal and what it represents, a primer on the magnitude of what that means, and how we can align with this in our shadow work. We do shadow work to achieve what the seal represents. Enjoy, learn something new to further validate your work using this book, your shadow work, healing yourself, wanting more in your life, and wanting to connect with your tribe and community! It's a collective shift, lean the fuck in, love each other and maybe even go live in nature on some land.

Fig. 19. "Aquarius Seal: Anthroposophy, Central Europe." *Symbolikon,* https://symbolikon.com/downloads/aquarius-seal-anthroposophy/.

Figure 19. Shows The Aquarius Seal, a symbolic emblem of the Age of Aquarius in Anthroposophical philosophy. For Anthroposophists, the Aquarian Seal brings the awakening of humanity to its cosmic belonging. Aquarius has the energies of enlightenment, community, and spiritual science. Culturally, the seal represents the beginning of the era where the outdated paradigms begin to crumble. Collective consciousness continues to grow as we connect with our shared divine essence. Bringing along with it utopian innovation and solutions to the world's issues (Aquarius Seal, n.d.).

I wanted to share with you a brief practice you can do to attune to the seal to activate its energetic vibration and lessons within you as we enter the new age. Daily meditation practice on the seal is recommended for best results. "Anthroposophy[8] utilizes the multidimensional Aquarius Seal to attune practitioners to the cosmic currents steering individual and collective spiritual evolution. Contemplating its symbols provides access to higher wisdom supporting human ascension," (Aquarius Seal, n.d.). We're evolving and I'm so happy you're here for it. Know that I'm teary-eyed as I write this, because I mean it.

When engaging in self-talk, you should try employing the below tips:

- Speak out loud
- **Reliability and Consistency**: If you desire long-lasting or second-order change in how you feel and perceive reality, then you have to be consistent and reliable when meeting with your shadows. By meeting with your shadows, I mean having an emotionally intelligent direct conversation with your shadow and fulfilling what was discussed and mutually agreed upon in the agreement made during your guided meditation. You're taking on the responsibility of role modeling to your shadow parts what healthy, supportive, loving, compassionate, empathetic and kind attachment, communication and relationship

---

[8] Anthroposophy is a spiritual philosophy and science that studies the human being and the relationship between the physical and spiritual worlds.

feels, looks, and functions like. You're healing the lived experience of relationships with yourself in this work. A lot of us have abandonment wounds, trauma, and shadow that we have to be mindful of when we're navigating life and doing our shadow work.

- **Get curious and ask yourself these questions:** From a non-judgmental place, implore the curiosity of a child, remain open. Why would you deny meeting any of your own needs first? If you don't have your back, why should anyone else? If you can't have your own back and care about yourself, why would others think you're trustworthy enough to care about them if you don't care enough about yourself? You can only love and meet others as deeply as you love and meet yourself. That experience can be rich and full of color, freedom, and so much love if you allow it to flow in from you and through you, to you, and everywhere else.

- **Know the age of the shadow you are talking to:** If you don't know specifically, guess. Trust what you feel or hear internally. You will be able to get a feel of the age range based on the level of emotional maturity felt in the behavior and intensity of the emotions and how it makes you want to behave. What thoughts may come to mind as far as how that energy makes you want to do and feel? Journal and keep track as you evolve.

- **Depending on what age your shadow self is you will speak to it in that tone of voice**: Use specific language, and statements that are appropriate for that age. I know this is awkward and it seems silly and uncomfortable. It may even feel stupid and like a waste of time. Your ego only impacts you and if your life doesn't improve, check to see how you were talking to that younger part of you. Do it even if you feel embarrassed and silly at first, keep going. Observe your experience and what you're doing and thinking, try to be mindful and aware if you're not feeling great. Does it feel teenagery and angsty, confrontational, like too cool for you, or intensely emotional? Do you want to have a temper tantrum and lip pout, scream, or cry? You might try sacred rage for both. Your tone of voice and the words you use are going to change depending on how old your shadow is. For a six-year-old shadow, you might call it a temper tantrum versus a rage release. One with cursing and one without.

- **Be in a private space alone and close your eyes:** It helps to get into the wise, loving, empathetic parent state of mind.

- **You must be real:** When you talk to your shadows—none of that postcard shit you get on a coffee mug. "You're the best! Go You! I'm so proud of you! I love you." If you have never said anything like that to yourself before, how do you think it's going to land out of nowhere? You'll get irritated because you don't believe it and don't think you ever will. It isn't authentic. Even if you keep trying, it's likely nothing will improve. Did you become a robot? Have you never met you before?

- **Go deep enough**: People have a tendency to be afraid of getting vulnerable with themselves. You might reject going deep enough, and deny what you're needing to hear or feel from yourself. When you finally say the things that make you tear up, it hits differently and you'll understand what I mean about going deep enough.

- **Cry**: Let yourself cry, please! Stop apologizing for your tears, hiding them, being embarrassed by them, hating crying in front of others, sucking your tears back in, looking tough, and "keeping it together." Stop doing all of that toxic unhealthy shit. Crying is pure magikal alchemy.

It takes your energetic emotion and alchemizes it into tears to then release out of your body. It's incredible and crying is the fastest way your body releases cortisol, the hormone that creates stress. Yes, when we're stressed we cry. When you're mad, sad, disappointed, stressed, overwhelmed, frustrated, anxious; cry. Your body is doing what it's supposed to do, which is regulate itself by pushing foreign material like stress out of your body. Let it happen.

- **Never underestimate the power of self-talk:** It will emotionally impact you in terms of making you feel warm and cared about. It might also make you a little sad, but that's okay and to be expected. It might cause a lot of complex feelings that lead you to burst into tears because you needed to hear that so badly from yourself. That's alright, let it all out, and be so grateful to yourself for being brave enough to say what you needed to hear, which was ultimately the truth you hid away from yourself in the shadows.

- **Never give tough love**: Never judge, criticize, say, or think you're a problem that needs fixing, or that there's something wrong with you.

- **Don't give up on yourself:** It will begin to feel and be different, just give it a little trust, space, and time.

- **You've programmed your life for how many years up to this point?** Give yourself some grace, if you're trying to flip the script in five seconds that's unrealistic. We're the stress and instant satisfaction generation, remember? We want immediacy but that desire for immediacy creates frustration, stress, and anger—a vortex of energy that overrides what you're really trying to accomplish, and keeps it further from you.

- **The real trick seems counterintuitive**: The more you surrender to whatever life brings to you without trying to control it every second, the more you start to be a true student of life. You're learning, experiencing, and flowing with what comes to you or is shown to you. For example, if you're still stuck in a shadow program of fear and scarcity, you'll be holding on for dear life, until you realize that if you let go of that identity, you can change your energetic relationship to it through the way you think about it. You can move towards acceptance by shifting your perspective. Try some of these statements: "Whatever happens, whatever's meant for me will come no matter what." Or "I (we to include your shadows) have everything that I need and I'm never without." Also, "I have all the time I need." Then, all of a sudden everything will start coming to you, once you match that energy of surrender, acceptance, and flow.

- **Be kind, compassionate, and patient with yourself:** This is part of getting real with yourself, the part where you see the bias to want to say 'I'll be patient with myself,' while also saying that you'll do it perfectly every time and never have any slip-ups. That couldn't be further from the truth, and every person's experience with it is different. What *is* consistent across the board is that every single person takes steps forward and one step back. This happens in cycles because there are lessons that you haven't learned yet that return to give you another opportunity. Then, the jumps become bigger, like ten steps forward and two steps back. Eventually, you get to a place of resonance with yourself and the energy that you want to exist in, flowing with what is. That's when you've reprogrammed what you can with what you're aware of and life is good. You can navigate it on your own. This doesn't mean you won't have new shadows you become aware of as your awareness expands, or trauma and life happens as it does. What it does mean, though, is you have the skills to navigate it and be the best friend, parent, child, and lover you can be for yourself. When you can be that for you, everyone else benefits, the collective and the world benefits. When you're regulating your nervous system and meeting your emotional needs on a regular basis, you don't have big reactions and feelings to things because you're operating from a more grounded baseline.

- **The goal is not to be grounded and calm 100% of the time:** You're not a robot. If we didn't get dysregulated or upset, we wouldn't know if we were in harm, or if someone crossed a boundary. Our nervous system keeps us safe and needs to do its job, so being able to return back to grounding is the key. As you practice the grounding skills to program them in, you'll naturally become more grounded, but you won't be practicing them all the time. Make more room for life to happen. Being able to ground yourself when your nervous system is dysregulated will amplify positive thoughts of yourself and improve your self-talk.

- **Ask them to look through your eyes:** If your shadow is dysregulated or if you feel them coming up with no triggering event, ask out loud for your shadow to look through your eyes to ground in the present moment. You will also need to ask your shadow to look through your eyes if they request to do a fun activity with you as part of bonding and feeling good like dancing or walking in nature. To make sure your shadows receive that healing and feel included you must invite them.

Example of how to talk to your shadow:

Let's say it's your seventeen-year-old self, rather than saying that aforementioned shit, you'll instead say, 'Listen, I know we don't know each other that well, even though we've been occupying the same home. I didn't know you were in there needing me, I'm so sorry. That must have been really painful and made you angry to not feel heard. I didn't know that was possible. Take my hand, let's get you out of that horrible place, memory, and person. I'm bringing you to safety here to live with me in the home we have together as an adult. Look through my eyes and see our place, I think you will love it here." Bond, connect, relate, validate, support, give space, and empowerment mixed in with some blind, unconditional love.

Continue the conversation to say, "I can feel you getting upset right now and I'm not sure why. I wasn't paying attention to what was happening, but I know the story of this feeling. I'm really sorry you're feeling this way. In case no one has ever told you before, it's okay to feel sad and lonely. We can allow ourselves to feel it without telling ourselves a story about it and that we have to fix it because it's uncomfortable or intense. We can just feel it and release it, letting it flow through us. I won't abandon you by focusing on toxic distractions and perpetuating the pattern. I'm here whether you like it or not. I've had to deal with you whether I liked it or not, now I know that you exist, it's an equal playing field. I will sit with you and tell you how dope and beautiful you are every time. I'll be sad with you. Then, we're going to shake it off and send that energy into the Earth to be transmuted into pure potential. I'm going to help us focus on what we can keep doing to help ourselves feel less sad and lonely and to help us finally be in alignment with what fulfills us and fills us up with joy, love, and gratitude. If we want that, we need to work together to feel and help ourselves by seeing the value and lessons in all things. We're reprogramming our minds for success and abundance, not scarcity anymore. We're not lacking in anything. We have everything we need! It's going to take time and feel strange at times, but when we get to the other side, we'll wonder why it took us so long to surrender to the process. But we'll be so grateful we did! Thank you for being a part of me and allowing me to feel you and honor you."

Example of how to talk to different aged shadow parts:

If you were talking to a seventeen-year-old version of you, you may be swearing more or trying to appear cool and likable to your teenage self who you know is pissed off and distrusting. When I was seventeen-year-old, I used to be so hard on myself, which caused me to act even more unhinged and distrusting. I felt so much rage and anger at my parents for moving us away from home to Kansas, and for killing my social life, because I acted out and was grounded all the time. I didn't feel safe with myself, let alone anyone else. I betrayed myself constantly then, but I didn't know that's what I was doing. My self-talk sounded like the above example.

Compare that to a six-year-old me, who was obsessed with jewelry and animals (nothing has changed there). I enjoyed playing outside and sleeping with my stuffed animals. I was innocent, sweet, gullible, genuinely loving and caring, and had the biggest heart that I gave freely. I wasn't afraid of anything, I had so much courage. I wasn't easily embarrassed and I would perform singing, dancing, and acting for anyone who would watch. I wanted to be seen by everyone and I knew I was worthy of being seen. With that said, I was a highly sensitive child with *enormous* emotions that I didn't know how to regulate nor did my family, Goddess bless them. I was a lot at times—the *drama*. My parents did their best, but my feelings would get hurt so easily if I didn't feel included, invited, or liked by others. I also couldn't be away from my mom for too long or I'd bawl uncontrollably and call for her until she would ultimately be called to come pick me up from a friend's house or school. I needed more nurturing than anyone knew how to handle.

As I got older, I got colder due to the trauma I didn't heal, but I chose the journey of unraveling that while reconnecting with the light within me. My inner child was once again filled with wonder and sparks of joy. I know that if my six-year-old shows up she needs a lot of loving, motherly self-talk, physical touch, or hugging myself and rocking, and rubbing as a self-soothing grounding tool as I speak to her out loud.

I say things like, "Hey cutie, come sit on my lap. Let me hold you (wrapping my arms around my body). I'm sorry you feel so upset and disappointed. It's okay to cry and let it out or feel rage because you feel hurt. I will patiently move aside and let you release it in a sacred rage release or we can get on the ground and pitch a fit. I will patiently wait for you to be ready to talk about it. I'm so proud of you for using your voice and telling me what you need and how you feel." Then I'll rage out or cry, whatever I need to come back to a grounded space where I have more clarity to know what might have triggered her.

I would say, "Okay, thank you for feeling your feelings and getting that out. What upset you? I'm sorry you feel that way. I understand how it may feel like they don't care, but I know that's not true. This person is not the same person who hurt us in the past. I'm here to protect you now. I wouldn't let anything like that or anyone like that in our lives again. It's okay if you don't trust me yet, but I will keep showing up for you and reminding you that I always got you[9]."

---

[9] My shadows respond to me directly. You may need to try automatic writing to get responses if you're attempting this without seeing a professional.

CHAPTER 8

COMMUNICATION & BOUNDARIES

One of the most valuable things I carried with me from my former days as a therapist, is the concept of making a conscious effort to communicate and set boundaries.

Shadow work is focused and isolated work, but it always has a direct impact on your relationships. You will need to know how to communicate your needs and expectations, as well as what the other person can expect if your shadow comes up in conversation or interactions in the future. I have included the **QR code** for the boundaries and communication form PDF in the resources section, or you can find it on my website (journeyofshadows.com/resources).

We came into this world in a society that tells us not to feel our feelings, to hide them, deny, or reject them. We're supposed to apologize for them and intellectually ruminate on them, which only increases the disconnection from our emotions and body. We were raised by a generation that values productivity and profit margins over everything else, alway staying busy so as not to sit still enough to think or feel. This is shadow's anxious-avoidant coping mechanism.

In short, we weren't taught how to effectively talk about our feelings and problems in a healthy way. Most of us probably didn't have a lot of healthy or good experiences with these subjects growing up. It makes a lot of sense why, as a collective, a lot of us don't know how to speak about what's going on with us or our emotions—especially boundaries if we've never had them.

You have to know your emotions and your needs in order to set boundaries. That's not something that was role-modeled for most of us, as the term "boundary" is a fairly new concept to many. I love helping people feel their feelings, honor, release, and alchemize them into pure potential. I've taken my communicating boundaries form and included all of the questions on it below for you to use as you please.

Communicating Boundaries Questions

You're getting clear on why you're having the conversation to begin with.

How does it apply to the person / why they need to know you're doing shadow work?

How would you describe to this person why you're doing shadow work?

How does it benefit them or your relationship? Why would they care or support this?

How could they support you in your shadow work? What are your needs from them?

What expectations do you have of them? How would you describe those boundaries?

How will you communicate your needs or bring in safety and trust that they can rely on for security?

How will you make sure to continue meeting your own needs as you involve others in your work?

If you've been utilizing the Daily Check-ins PDF list and consistently practicing your grounding and coping skills, you took the time to experiment and test which skills helped which emotion and trigger best so you can have a fast-track grounding first aid tool kit. This also allows you to be able to communicate this to whomever.

Next time you discuss your emotions and articulate honestly with confidence, feeling unconcerned about the opinions of others, it's so empowering! This is a form of independence that will make you feel truly proud. It might make you emotional because of how far you've come, or because of how grateful you are to yourself, for caring so much about all parts of you that you set special boundaries because you love and care about them. They are important and need you, you are there to help your shadow selves.

You are here to help your own self. You need to worry less about what everyone else is concerned about and what other people need and more about what you need.

As people, let's invest less in pop culture, stop limiting ourselves by listening only to mainstream media, and not hold ourselves back for fear of being misunderstood. I hope my message is clear enough by now, but do what you want, go after what you want. Live your life, experience it—or settle for an unfulfilled existence. It's your choice to do what you want with the information I provide. Take what works, leave what doesn't.

Remember to get specific about your self-talk expectations with your partner or whoever. Give them a whole breakdown, or better yet, I suggest reading them off the page, if possible. I know that can be a big step for some of you and I honor that. I'm only asking you to meet yourself where you're at, but you've got to challenge yourself at a certain point or there won't be movement or growth happening.

As previously mentioned, each shadow and its trigger will require different ways of meeting emotional needs. That may lead you to request more physical touch and cuddling for your younger shadow who feels abandoned. That might look like requesting to not talk much for a while, or maybe just a silent embrace until you're grounded and feeling safe in your body, then you can talk about it.

Remember to be mindful of what is healthy, in balance, within reason/fairness, and that you're not taking advantage of, manipulating, or abusing your power or control. See to it that you're being empathetic to their feelings and emotional needs as well. Your boundaries are made to honor your needs first, but you need to know that it's not coming from your shadow self.

When you're triggered and you're in shadow, you won't know your boundaries or true emotional needs unless you've practiced this a lot and done the inner work to find out. It's key to be mindful and empathetic of others' experiences as well.

We can all be manipulative or codependent in some way, shape, or form, whether we're aware of it or not. Certain shadows we come across may bring out more difficult emotions that are tricky to sit with, emotions that bring up shadow programs of manipulative or codependent patterns that were used in survival mode to get out of uncomfortable situations in you or your family's past. It's a matter of knowing if that's a shadow of yours. If it's a pattern to manipulate others, in even the smallest of ways that you would normally try to excuse, then acceptance and validation are appropriate.

An example of manipulation while triggered is using your sexuality to control another person's emotions in order to avoid accountability for consequences or to lighten the blow. Another example is when feelings of abandonment trigger a pattern of codependency to come online, and instead of acknowledging it as a shadow pattern, you will unconsciously do what it wants you to do, like have your partner with you constantly to help you ground or self-soothe.

There's nothing wrong with having your partner or whoever is helping you self-soothe, but the goal is to be able to do this for yourself. If it's your natural inclination to involve your partner in every aspect of your life without separation, you'll want to look into the shadow of codependency. Needing help every now and then is okay, and spending time together and building a life together is beautiful, but there's a level of individuality that must be met. You're individuals living separate realities and you must honor your own needs, wants, and desires. Don't expect one person to meet all of your needs.

If you can never do anything on your own and don't even try, that's when a connection might be toxic and considered unhealthy. The purpose is to empower you to first try to self-soothe on your own, and when you need others, then you lean on them. But you should know how to show up for yourself first and foremost.

Remember that in shadow work, we're identifying shadow, which is anything not supporting your highest good and the highest good of all. So when you're introspecting and doing those journal prompts to better understand your need and desire for boundaries, it's important to be aware of what you might not have conscious awareness of.

The example I give at the end of the chapter may seem obvious when reading it, but when it's your life, there's a strong urge to deny things that make you look unfavorable or not in your highest good. Some people are very honest with themselves, but still have limitations around what they have conscious access to. If you're not working with a professional who can take you to an altered state of consciousness, then I would suggest you ask friends, family, and partner(s) that you trust who can give you honest feedback and truth about your behavior. It's important to remain open to whatever is said to you, because you'll likely want to deny it.

Cross-reference among individuals if you need to (ask friends and family to pay attention to that behavior you might be doing and to let you know) because you're having a hard time accepting the truth. If it comes out a resounding 'yes, you do this thing,' it's going to be okay. The world will not end and you're not a demon who is going to burn in hell for not being aware that you're incredibly rude sometimes when you're upset, with a tendency to manipulate anyone around you sexually to get out of facing it.

Forgive yourself, you're a beautiful spirit who knows growth has to happen here. Face the music so you can create an informed and truthful set of boundaries that resonate for all involved. Ask others to review them with you before presenting them to your partner or whoever. Bring awareness to any manipulation or codependency to further help you clarify these behaviors and reach a greater understanding of healthy boundaries.

This job of meeting your emotional needs, using grounding and coping skills, using loving self-talk, communicating your needs, and setting boundaries are yours and yours alone. Whoever you choose can be by your side or in the background or the other room as your protector and safety, but they're not your problem solver, fixer, or punching bag.

You are your helper and powerful healer, not your partner or any other person who you discuss this work with. Remember this empowering statement I tell every client: "No one can make you feel anything. You make yourself feel everything. No one has that kind of power over you, except your mind." I don't know where I heard it, maybe during graduate school, but I added some of my own words. You aren't asking much of the other person beyond respect, privacy, trust, empathy, and patience.

The process of setting boundaries and learning how to communicate them is simplified via the boundary setting form.

You can use it as much as you want. You will begin to know your triggers and emotions better, and you will begin to see shadows more easily. You'll soon learn to quickly identify the specific shadow, its age, the emotion it's connected to, and what grounding and coping skills help with that emotion. You'll begin to learn how your shadow wants you to meet those emotional needs. Then, you'll work on how to protect that process of you showing up to meet those needs and the boundaries you create. How do you want to keep this practice sacred? You're not asking for permission. You are stating what they can expect. What's happening and why, and how can they support you if you want them to?

You will begin to see boundaries as opportunities for growth and to lean in on the good feelings. You're doing good things for you because it feels good.

Maybe you'll begin to notice that when your partner gets home from hanging out with friends, he's all pumped up and hyper. It annoys you. You might come off as rude and disinterested. Your partner accuses you of being upset that he went out without you.

You, on the other hand, have been at home chilling all evening after yoga, a meditation practice, and your ritual bath. You feel very zen, but can't handle the high energy clash when he boulders through the door.

There's a need for a boundary if he has been out with friends, and you're happy for him, but the high energy is irritating when you're feeling zen. An example of setting a boundary so you're able to show up and be supportive in the way you want to be for him, is to ask him to text when he's coming home with where his energy level is at. If he is still pumped up, you can go into the bedroom with the door closed and text something like "goodnight babe, let's talk in the morning."

Then, he can have the house to himself to wind down and only come into the bedroom when his energy level dissipates. If you practice boundaries in this way, both members of the couple will notice that it helps maintain emotional balance and avoids unnecessary shadow arguments.

It may be a bummer at first to not see a partner right when they return home after dinner, but when you remember why you'll be grateful. Now, neither of you have to feel guilty for being yourselves. You can be yourself freely, accepting and loving each other as separate people living separate lives that don't always dovetail together on exactly the same wavelength, energy level, or mood.

Our society has a shadow program that says we're all supposed to like the same things or want the same things, or that life only looks one or two ways. When, really, it could look infinite. Open your mind to see what could be possible. Your shadow may not see how things can work out or what a partnership can look like.

This is where some people can get stuck in shadows, because they don't see that the relationship they're trying to save, control, or force is toxic and isn't meant to work out. Surrender to what is. We only allow in what we feel we are worthy of.

If your partner makes you feel low self-worth, low self-esteem, powerlessness, or anything other than spectacular and amazing, it's not serving your highest good. If your therapist and best friend won't say it, I will. Leave your abusive husband or wife or partner. Leave anything that does not make you feel worthy of everything precious under the sun, moon, and stars.

Bless their life, they may not be aware. It isn't your business. You don't have to leave things in a nasty way, sometimes you leave and never look back.

Often bigger and better things don't come to us because we don't dare to dream big enough as a byproduct of the collective shadow programming that's been conditioned into us through oppression, fear, and abuse. Try to avoid blaming language or accusing language and saying things like "you do this or you do that." Focus on yourself and say things like "I feel like" or "I'm noticing I feel this when this happens." Try not to interrupt each other. Give space for each person to speak, or end the conversation until both parties can speak with truth, integrity, and respect.

The same rule applies to staying calm and not arguing. You can disagree and speak with respect without yelling and calling each other names or putting each other down. You can each be upset and feel your feelings without talking over each other in order to "win."

Maybe try doing somatic exercises together like shaking, sacred rage release (privately if this would be triggering), or breathwork before beginning the conversation about what just happened and why. Read the room and feel into it, if the energy gets tense and intense, take a break and return when you're both feeling more grounded. Learning healthy balance in communication and energy tolerance will get you far in maintaining healthy communication within your relationships.

If your partner has an issue supporting you in your shadow work, then you have every right to be upset. Of course, they don't have to support you in it. That's their choice, and you can't make anyone do anything, but you would hope that the person you're communicating your boundaries to also wants what's best for you, and ultimately the relationship.

If they aren't okay with you setting boundaries, that's a *huge* red flag and shouldn't be overlooked. Try to gain greater clarity on what about your boundaries upsets them, or what they don't like about them? Inquire what would make it feel better for them? If what they have to say is reasonable and understandable and you're still able to meet your emotional needs, negotiate a compromise that feels good to both of you. Don't sacrifice meeting your needs. If that's what's being asked of you, this person doesn't have your best interests in mind.

If your partner is not supportive because of a lack of control over you, or because you're becoming more empowered, break up with or divorce this person *immediately*. Of course, you don't have to listen to anything I tell you, or believe anything I say either. If anyone in your life doesn't respect your boundaries and is offended by you setting them, they don't have your best interests at heart. They want to see you fail, lose, suffer, or be powerless.

Go be with yourself to heal, you deserve that and so much more. It will be even more amazing when you eventually meet the person who will thrive with you in your empowerment. There are so many people who will radiate joy and pride to see you happy, and help you reach your full potential and maximum abundance.

Choosing yourself may feel impossible to do, especially if you've never chosen yourself before. It might also make you very afraid, but that happens every time we leave something and enter into something better. Things have to leave your life for better stuff to come in.

Would you rather never do anything, be miserable, and wonder *what if?* Or would you rather see the truth, change your life, and be able to experience what you truly desire because you choose to be an active, healing-conscious participant in your life? Trust and believe that what leaves is meant to go. Say, "Good riddance, and thank you for teaching me so I can be closer to my truth and my heart's greatest desires, I release you."

There's a collective shadow program we've all been fed about what relationships look like and our attachment to that ideal creates our core beliefs and values about relationships.

We say things like "forever" and "as long as we both shall live" which doesn't give room for life to happen. It doesn't honor the natural ebbs and flows of life. These promises can create unrealistic mind prisons and rules about who we are as people within these relationships.

We're entering a new age where we lean into what's real and honest for each of us. I don't mean that marriage will become obsolete or that people will start getting divorced or wanting open marriages. I feel that we're shifting towards viewing relationships differently because we're viewing ourselves in relation to others differently.

People want only that which brings growth, positivity, joy, and love into their lives to remain. Release the idea that we can control anything and that we no longer work from our wounds. Try to feel grateful for the relationships that are healthy, and continue to be grateful even if one ends with no new beginnings in sight. Be grateful for whatever time you had together and the lessons you learned from the connection as it's a part of your ever-evolving being.

An example of a boundary conversation sounds like this:

"I'm not sure if you've heard me mention my shadow work, but I'm learning about my hidden emotions and thoughts and how they affect me by becoming more aware of them. I'm helping myself feel my emotions without projecting them onto others. When triggers come up I would appreciate your support in my shadow work because it will improve our relationship on many levels. If I get mad I may not be able to say a whole lot in fear that I may yell at you or say things I don't mean. So, if I awkwardly turn red, glare at you with my left eyebrow up, or avoid eye contact and storm out of the room by slamming my door, that means I'm doing shadow work. This means I'm mad, so I'll be doing a sacred rage release. I'll be screaming and hitting my pillow on the bed. Please don't come in or check on me. My anger is not at you. Please respect my privacy and space. If you want to leave the house that's great too. I will text you at the end of the day or when I feel ready to talk about it. If I don't feel ready yet, then I'll let you know that night and text you the next day and keep going like that until I'm ready to talk about it. I will communicate when I can and not leave you hanging. When I'm triggered, I can't communicate much in the moment yet, so this is what I can do for now until I have a greater window of tolerance built, or I finally release and alchemize that shadow's wound."

CHAPTER 9

THERE IS NO DESTINATION

Fig. 20. "Unveiling the Mysteries of the Subconscious Mind: A Journey Within." *English Plus Podcast*, Danny Ballan, images.app.goo.gl/4sSUavhtCzEsqDjm6

More repetition means you're more likely to remember the information. That may be why I've repeated myself so many times in this book—to help you remember. As I've told you, there is no destination. There's no end goal, there's no timeframe to be healed or move through shadow work. It's always evolving work that stops, pauses, and starts again.

We live 90 to 95 percent in the shadows, yet there's so much information in our brains that we have no idea how to access, and quite a bit of information we don't want access to, like internal bodily processes of digestion or our heart beat.

As you continue to responsibly honor yourself by doing this sacred work, make sure to take breaks to reset emotionally when you feel called to. Play. Have fun. Don't take life so seriously. Do all of the above while integrating the lessons, even during a break from shadow work.

You may be taking a break from shadow work, but you did recently uncover various information in your shadow work that you're working to integrate into changed behavior or thoughts, etc. You're still actively working to pull that into your awareness and do the best you can to create some form of changed behavior, even if that just means you're using grounding and coping skills when you feel irritated. Maybe you recently discovered that's something you need, as you've been experimenting to see what best helps you with what.

The idea that your shadows are healed and each of them is released, and what's left is only love and light is unrealistic. We're spirits living in this human existence, and we will always have shadows because of duality. It's the opposing forces of light and dark that define the experience of this dimension on Earth.

Yes, shadow work will help you heal your trauma and release the wounds of your past. It can teach you to learn how to honor, love, and express all of your emotions without a story, and without narratives of the past overshadowing what's meant to happen. Allow yourself to feel an emotion, let it move through your body and out into the ground. Emotions are information about your environment that your shadow brain uses to keep you safe when someone has crossed a boundary or hurt you. But it originates from the past. It's how you protect yourself and survive.

Your shadows are not your weakness, they're your strength, your power, and your wisdom. We must learn how to harness those emotions by providing them that necessary outlet so we can communicate how we truly mean to. It's only when we're in shadow and haven't released all of our pent-up emotional energy that we're unable to communicate the truth. There might be edges of shadow in the response, and it may pass by you and others, but you will feel it in your body.

You're meant to have both light and dark, you can't be one without the other. If someone portrays themselves that way, it's an illusion. In that case, one is in denial of their darkness, which is another way of being in shadow. True wisdom and power comes from walking between the worlds of light and dark. I'm of the light, giving light and love to my darkness, and acting as a torch leading it back to the true path, like Goddess Hecate. I don't see my anger or rage as bad or negative. I honor it and give it sacred room to express and be freed so that it doesn't unleash on those it isn't meant for. I give myself sacred space to feel it and move through it, becoming wild and free through sacred rage release.

You will learn your unique dance that will also evolve and shift, learning when to surrender and when to challenge yourself, when to just listen and be rather than doing and thinking.

You will evolve as your shadow work, needs, desires, and connections have evolved. You will transform into newer, truer versions of yourself, meaning your boundaries and shadow work will also change to reflect that.

If you're getting stuck and not evolving, or feeling stagnant in your shadow work, then it can be a few different things. It could be that you're not processing, you're ruminating and further ingraining the shadow program, which is working against what you're trying to do. When we are truly processing it's a thought cycle that has an end point at a new perspective of the same situation, creating a different emotional experience in relation to it.

Another reason could be that you aren't speaking to yourself in the way you need, maybe you're not being vulnerable or going deep enough. If you don't hear exactly what you need to hear in the way you need to hear it, that's probably because saying what you need to hear makes you uncomfortable. It might make you cry in the tone of voice and words your six-year-old shadow needs to hear it.

You also may not be aware of or catch all of your negative self-talk about yourself or the situations you're having trouble in. Or, you got comfortable and stopped challenging yourself to grow further due to other shadows. It's the shadow dance of layers of shadows upon shadows.

The reason why you're not making the progress you want, you're stuck, or not feeling different in your shadow work, is because different shadows of yours are blocking you from healing the other ones. That's when you must look into what hidden beliefs, thoughts, and feelings that might be there that want to block you from X, Y, and Z.

That's where you'll find a lot of the collective, ancestral, generational, and past life trauma, as shadow programs blocking you from your abundance and joy. It's typically the bigger, overarching conditioned collective programs that linger since those aren't tied directly to your current life.

Therefore, it might take some time to conclude that you need a professional, a shaman, or a specialist to take you into an altered state of consciousness to heal and remove any unwanted blocks that are no longer yours to carry. This only works if you're aware that collective shadow programs and past life, generational, and ancestral trauma are real. Only then will you be able to remove said blocks to access your abundance.

If you don't know that this kind of trauma exists, and can show up as not believing in yourself and going after your dreams, you won't reach your full potential, because you won't be aware that there's an ancestral contract directly blocking your abundance. With time, dedicated research, and an open mind, you'll eventually come across this concept and be willing to address it. Knowledge is power. Awareness is a gift that we can't do anything important without.

This will be a journey that you can choose to learn to enjoy, and lean into. Think of the journey itself as your trusted teacher who will never give you a lesson you're not worthy of or that's too difficult for you to complete.

My hope is not to precipitate feelings of discouragement, but instead inspire you to enjoy the ride, because there's something to be grateful for and learn from in every stage of your evolution, trauma, challenge, and shadow. It will become less about a destination and more about seeing the hidden truths and answers in plain sight. In all situations, having an inside scoop into your life, with the ability to master supporting yourself and your needs, is going to feel incredible. You'll be communicating and creating boundaries, and becoming your own wise protective Gandalf. You deserve to feel that wisdom, protection, and safe trust within yourself.

Doing shadow work is worth it. You are worth it. You deserve to get more out of life, and to experience it more fully and freely, on your own terms, and in your own way. This work will help you become more alive. I hope you set yourself free of the programs and conditioning that isn't yours. Release yourself from all the heavy burdens you no longer need to carry. I hope you revel in the wild, raw, beautiful force that you are and know that you are powerful beyond measure. I hope you know that your life can begin anew any day at any age and that you can make a different choice at any moment.

I hope you know that you're already free and you already have everything you need. I hope you know how unique and special you are, and how lucky we are to have your magik and essence be a part of this world. I'm so happy, grateful, and honored to be on this Earth with you. Thank you for choosing to live this life and for allowing me to share my journey and wisdom with you. As always, take what you like and leave what you don't like.

I hope in this life you feel peace and so much abundant joy, light, love, pleasure, fun, success, money, friends, community, connection, and expansiveness in your opportunities and experiences. I honor you. I love you and all of your dark edges. Blessed be.

BIBLIOGRAPHY

Akinrodoye, M. A., & Lui, F. (2022)."Neuroanatomy, Somatic Nervous System." *National Library of Medicine: National Center for Biotechnology Information.* [Internet]. StatPearls Publishing, 7 Nov 2022, https://www.ncbi.nlm.nih.gov/books/NBK556027/#:~:text=The%20so matic%20nervous%20system%20is,legs%2C%20and%20other%20bo dy%20parts. Accessed 14 Feb 2024.

Cayce, Edgar. The Akashic Records: Blueprint for Your Soul. A.R.E. Press, 2020.

Cherry, Kendra. "How the Peripheral Nervous System Works." *VeryWellMind,* https://www.verywellmind.com/what-is-the-peripheral-nervous-system-2795465. Accessed 3 May 2024.

Gustafson, Craig. "Bruce Lipton, PhD: The Jump From Cell Culture to Consciousness." *Integrative Medicine: A Clinician's Journal,* Vol. 16(6), InnoVision Health Media Inc, 2017, Encinitas, CA. 44-50. PMCID: PMC6438088; PMID: 30936816.

Herrera, S. N., Sarac, C., Phili, A., Gorman, J., Martin, L., Lyallpuri, R., Dobbs, M. F., Deluca, J. S., Mueser, K. T., Wyka, K. E., Yang, L. H., Landa, Y., Corcoran, C. M. (2023). Psychoeducation for Individuals at Clinical High Risk for Psychosis: A Scoping Review. *Schizophrenia Research*, 252, 148-158. https://doi.org/10.1016/j.schres.2023.01.008

Howe, Linda. How to Read the Akashic Records: Accessing the Archive of the Soul and Its Journey. Sounds True, 2009.

Jacobsen, Jenni. "Signs of Repressed Childhood Trauma in Adults." *Nobu,* 6 June 2022, **https://www.nobu.ai/blog/childhood-trauma-in-adults/**. Accessed 4 February 2024.

Jung, Carl. *Aion: Researches Into The Phenomenology Of The Self.* Translated by R.F.C. Hull, Vol. 9, Pantheon Books, New York City, NY, 1959.

Kenny, B. J., & Bordoni, B. "Neuroanatomy, Cranial Nerve 10 (Vagus Nerve)." *National Library of Medicine: National Center for*

Biotechnology Information [Internet]. StatPearls Publishing. 2022 Nov 7, https://www.ncbi.nlm.nih.gov/books/NBK537171/?report=reader#!po =81.2500. Accessed 4 May 2024.

Molitor, Michele. "Neuroplasticity, The Science Behind Rapidly Rewiring Your Brain." *Linked In,* 14 Sept. 2019, https://www.linkedin.com/pulse/neuroplasticity-science-behind-rapidly-rewiring-your-michele/

Accessed 12 March 2024.

"Nervous System: What it is, Parts, Functions, and Disorders." *Cleveland Clinic,* https://my.clevelandclinic.org/health/body/21202-nervous-system. Accessed 4 May 2024.

"The Science of Brainwaves: The Language of The Brain." *Neurohealth*, 2024, https://nhahealth.com/brainwaves-the-language/

"Unconscious." *Psychology Today,* https://www.psychologytoday.com/us/basics/unconscious#:~:text=Th e%20unconscious%20is%20the%20vast,available%20to%20the%20c onscious%20mind. Accessed 30 Feb 2024.

"Understanding the Vagus Nerve." *Khiron Clinics, 9 Dec 2022.* https://khironclinics.com/blog/understanding-the-vagus-nerve/#:~:text=Traumatic%20experiences%20can%20contribute%20t o,vomiting%2C%20dizziness%20and%20abdomen%20pain.

"Understanding Trauma and The Nervous System: An Interconnected Web." *Orchestrate Health*, 12 Apr 2023. https://www.orchestratehealth.com/understanding-trauma-and-the-nervous-system-an-interconnected-web/. Accessed 22 Feb 2024.

Yehuda, R., & Lehrner, A. (2018). Intergenerational transmission of trauma effects: putative role of epigenetic mechanisms. *World Psychiatry*, 17(3): 243-257. https://doi:10.1002/wps.20568

Young, Emma. "Lifting The Lid On The Unconscious." *NewScientist: Humans*, 25 July 2018, https://www.newscientist.com/article/mg23931880-400-lifting-the-lid-on-the-unconscious/. Accessed 7 May 2024.

RESOURCES

Resources page for free grounding and coping skills, daily check-ins, guides, and more, all of which can be found on my website: www.journeyofshadows.com/resources

Scan **QR code** to access free coping & grounding skills:

"The Intention Experiment" by Lynn McTaggart

Dr. Masaru Emoto's Study of Water: Masaru Emoto Water Experiments. Scan QR code to watch!

"The Hidden Messages in Water" by Dr. Masaru Emoto

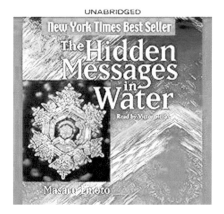

"The Shadow Work Journal: A Guide to Integrate and Transcend Your Shadows" by Keila Shaheen

ABOUT THE AUTHOR

Courtney Keiser is a former trauma-informed psychotherapist who chose to retire her license and create her own title that reflected additional valuable experience and skills as a Shadow Alchemist & Trauma Specialist. Courtney saw the missing links and missed opportunities within the limitations of psychotherapy, and noticed the treatment style often left clients feeling unfulfilled. Courtney noticed both she and her clients felt like there was something deeper that they wanted to know, a desire for true purpose and deeper meaning.

Taking action, Courtney journeyed into her underworld and fearlessly faced her own internal darkness and emotional wounds. She feared what she didn't have access to could be affecting her life. Now, she's spent over a decade working with various healers, mystics, intuitives, witches, shamans, therapists, and practitioners, combining all of that wisdom and still journeying ever deeper. Along the way, she gained several alternative healing certifications and initiations as she felt called to remember and reconnect to her ancient wisdom and medicine. Through these incredible facilitators and agents of healing, she remembered who she was.

Courtney's perspective is her gift to see shadow, to see what's hidden underneath, but also, all of the light within the person and situation as well. This lens enables her to see the higher meaning of what is transpiring in her client's lives and why. Courtney's one-of-a-kind guided meditation allows clients to directly engage with their shadow parts, and it's part of what makes the ASWM approach a game-changer for achieving emotional attunement within the self.

As she collected the pieces to the spiritual puzzle that became her approach, The Advanced Shadow Work Method, or ASWM, Courtney pulled in wisdom from magik, spirituality, psychotherapy, somatic practices, neurobiology, brain scan studies, reiki, and spiritual science. By combining influences from all these modalities, she was able to create ASWM, and has been successfully using it with clients for over six years. She's not recreating the wheel but building off what already exists by updating it with modern information.

Made in the USA
Columbia, SC
12 January 2025

51675651R00100